THE WIDENING GAP

THE
WIDENING
GAP

Why America's Working Families
Are in Jeopardy and
What Can Be Done About It

Jody Heymann

BASIC
BOOKS

A Member of the Perseus Books Group

Book design by Mark McGarry, Texas Type & Book Works
Set in Minion

Library of Congress Cataloging-in-Publication Data
Heymann, Jody, 1959–
The widening gap : why America's working families are in jeopardy and what can be done about it / Jody Heymann
          p. cm.
Includes bibliographical references and index.
ISBN 0-465-01308-2 (alk. paper)
1. Work and family—United States. I. Title.
HD4904.25 .H48 2000
306.85'0973—dc21
00-034298

00 01 02 03 / 10 9 8 7 6 5 4 3 2 1

To Benjamin, Jeremiah, and their generation

Contents

Equality is the public recognition effectively expressed in institutions and manners, of the principle that an equal degree of attention is due to the needs of all human beings.

SIMONE WEIL

CHAPTER ONE

Overview

AT 11 YEARS OLD, Andrew McAllister was left alone every week to care for his 5-year-old brother, Jonathan, after school.[1] Often they wandered the streets of a city where a child Andrew's age had recently been abducted and murdered during after-school hours. In another neighborhood, Karin Arnette returned to the only child care she could afford to find that her infant daughter had been left alone on a stripped mattress while the woman who was supposed to be looking after her slept. A father, Luis Marquez, took along both of his toddlers to his job interviews; he had to get a job if they were going to eat, and no publicly funded child care was available. Seven-year-old Jesse Olivarez, who had a learning disability, struggled in school and needed an adult to help him keep up with his class; but his single mother had to work evenings, and he was left alone with his 10-year-old brother. Elizabeth Carter ended up losing her job when she took leave too often to care for her daughter, Lucy, who had asthma. Situations like these are repeated every day all over the United States.

The overwhelming majority of children in this country are raised in households in which every adult works at a wage or salary job. Yet in spite of this, school days are usually two-thirds as long as typical workdays, the school year has 30 percent fewer days than the work year, and the need for out-of-school care far outstrips its availability. Leave from work to care for their children's health or to address critical educational issues is unavailable to tens of millions of Americans. Affordable, decent care for preschool children is available to fewer families than paid leave. Care for preschool children costs more than a state university education—and with far more limited financial aid.

Likewise, older Americans—whose numbers are rapidly rising—increasingly have only their children who are employed full-time to care for them. One in four U.S. families is responsible for taking care of elderly relatives; this number is mounting as both the absolute number of elderly and the proportion of the population that is elderly are swelling.[2] Yet there are few affordable services to help working Americans care for elderly parents.

The gap between caretaking demands and resources is large and growing. How did we as a nation reach this point, where programs and policies lag so dramatically behind families' needs?

A Revolution in Labor

In the past century and a half, two major transformations have changed the makeup of this country's labor force. The first, the movement of men out of agricultural and other home-based work into the paid industrial labor force, began in the 1840s. The second began in earnest a century later, when women entered wage and salary jobs in significant numbers.

From the founding of the United States until the mid-1800s, most children were raised in farm families in which both parents worked at home.[3] In 1830, 70 percent of children lived in farm families, and only 15 percent had a father who was a wage earner.[4] As the industrial revolution progressed, the number of families in which the father was a wage earner began to rise. In the 1880s, for the first time in U.S. history, being raised in a family in which the father earned a wage or salary outside the home and a mother did not was more common than being raised in a family in which two parents worked on a farm. By the 1920s, the majority of children were growing up in families in which the father worked outside the home,[5] and by 1930, only 30 percent lived in farm families.[6]

Although women had been among the first Americans to work in factories when the industrial revolution got under way in the early 1800s, unmarried women made up the majority of the women's labor force (see Figure A.1, Appendix A). Moreover, two-thirds of women stopped working when they married.[7] While women of color had begun working in the paid labor force before white women had, they too showed significantly different work patterns for single and married women. Not until the second half of the twentieth century did the majority of married nonwhite women work in paid jobs in the non-agricultural labor force.[8]

The limited labor force participation by married women in the 1800s and early 1900s was neither an accident nor a result of women's choices. Openings for men and women were advertised separately, many jobs barred women, many others explicitly barred married women, and employers could legally discriminate against women in hiring. It was not until World War II—when large numbers of women were needed to fill the jobs held by men who had gone to war—that a dramatic decline in discrimination against married women occurred in hiring.[9]

Just as marked changes in the employment of mothers of school-age

children began in the 1940s, equally marked changes in the employment of mothers of preschool children began in the 1960s (see Figure
A.2, Appendix A). By 1990, more than 70 percent of children lived in
households in which every parent was in the labor force.[10] Changes
in labor force participation permeated the experience of women
across the life span and led to profound changes in who was at home
to care for elderly parents as well as young children (see Figure A.3,
Appendix A).

By the end of the revolution in labor force participation, dramatic
changes had taken place in families. These changes were the result not
of women entering the wage and salary sector but rather of *both men
and women* entering the industrial and postindustrial labor force. The
fact that both men and women labor is not new. What has been altered
radically over the past 150 years for both men and women is the location and conditions of work. When most adults were working at their
homes or on their land, their children and adult family members in
need of care were with them, or nearby, as they worked. As the transformation in the location and nature of labor began, families became
dependent on wages and salaries for food, clothing, and other essen-
tials. By the end of the revolution, most families no longer had any
adult working at home full-time.

Society's Unfinished Response

In response to the beginning of the industrial revolution, American
communities, states, and the federal government recognized that if
lone wage earners were injured, lost their jobs, or grew too old or sick
to work, their families would lack money for food and clothing.
Consequently, a series of state and federal programs—workmen's
compensation, unemployment insurance, and old-age and survivors'
insurance—were created in the first third of the twentieth century to

ensure that families were cared for even if the single earner could no longer work.[11]

While men's entry into the labor force began to change how families met caretaking needs, women's entry into the labor force completed this transformation. But communities, states, and the federal government, in marked contrast to their responses to the first revolution in labor, have responded little to this second one, with its profound implications for the availability of adults to care for children and other dependents. The only federal government response has been to require large employers to offer unpaid family leave to a fraction of employees. Yet unpaid family leave is something most families cannot afford. Only a small percentage of corporations have made real changes beyond this mandated one. Meanwhile, what is expected of working families is increasing on many fronts. For example, to cut corporate health-care costs, children and adults with major health problems—who used to be cared for in the hospital—are now routinely sent home with the expectation that family members will somehow be able to take care of them. Likewise, whereas it was once understood that single parents living in poverty could not reasonably be expected to work full-time and simultaneously care well for their children without assistance, these parents are now expected to do both with next to no support.[12] Schedules that require evening or nighttime hours are more common, and work hours are increasing.[13]

Little or nothing has been done to answer the critical questions families are facing: Who cares for children during school vacations that can add up to five or seven times as much as their parents' paid leave from work? What happens to children when parents must work evenings and nights? Who cares for elderly parents who can no longer care for themselves? What happens when children and the elderly get sick and need care at unanticipated times? What happens when children have school problems and need adults' help? The revolutionary movement of men and women into the industrial and postindustrial labor force has transformed the United States. But we as a nation have failed to respond, leaving a rapidly widening gap between working families' needs and the combination of high workplace demands, outdated social institutions, and inadequate public policies.

Meeting Families' Needs

To tell the story of working families[14] in America—the whole story—it is essential to learn about poor families and rich families, truck drivers and doctors, single parents who have relatives readily available to help them, married parents who receive so little support from their spouses that they might as well be single, and families who live in communities that provide child care and after-school programs as well as those who live where there are few services. Working families in America are amazingly diverse in occupation, income, race, ethnicity, country of origin, and religion. They differ by who makes up a family: whether there are children being cared for, whether there are elderly grandparents being cared for or active grandparents providing care, whether there are disabled caregivers or care recipients, whether there are one or two parents present, and whether stepparents make the number of parents more than two.

Over the past seven years, I have built and led a research group devoted to examining the conditions faced by the entire range of working families living across the United States and to studying how those conditions affect the health, development, and welfare of families. Based at Harvard University, I have designed and led all the studies reported in this book. To reflect the efforts of the remarkable group of research assistants, students, and other team members I have had the privilege to lead, I often use the terms "we" and "our" to refer to my team's efforts. Nonetheless, for better or worse, the responsibility for the studies and the conclusions drawn from them rests with me.

The research group I lead has conducted both national and urban studies. Among the principal sources of data for this book are our Urban Working Families Study, a collaborative national Daily Diaries Study, the Department of Labor's National Longitudinal Survey of Youth (NLSY), and the Survey of Midlife in the United States. In the Daily Diaries Study, whose research was supported by the MacArthur Foundation, I developed questions for and analyzed the first systematic nationally representative study to daily ask more than eight hundred Americans, aged 25 to 74, across the country, whether they had to cut back on their work to meet family members' needs. In research supported by the National Institutes of Health and the William T. Grant Foundation, I analyzed extensive, nationally representative, longitudinal data from the NLSY on more than four thousand working parents to see whether parents had the paid leave or flexibility they needed to care for their children's health and development. And in research supported by a Picker Commonwealth scholarship, I developed an ethnographic urban study that involved in-depth interviews of representative samples of employers at their work sites, teachers at day-care centers, and urban families in their homes over the course of many months. These studies are described in detail in Appendix B.

Together, the studies on which this book is based involved interviews with more than 7,500 caregivers and included in-depth interviews in people's homes, daily diaries, testing of children, and multiyear follow-ups. They examine how Americans of all ages are working while addressing the health, educational, and routine- and urgent-care needs of children, elderly parents, and other adults. The studies provide an unprecedented view of what experiences working Americans share and how these experiences diverge by social class. They also provide some of the first evidence about how the health and development of our nation's children are being affected—often for the worse—by the current trends.

At the beginning of the twenty-first century, the United States has few community supports or social services designed to address anything other than preschoolers' routine daytime needs. But Americans often have evening, night, or weekend work and are caring for school-children, the elderly, and the disabled as well. Furthermore, whereas daily child-care needs are predictable, many other family needs, such as helping a hospitalized grandparent or a child failing at school, are not. Despite this fact, few researchers or policymakers have looked beyond the routine, nine-to-five, business-day needs of the young children of working parents. In Chapter 2, I discuss the results of the Daily Diaries Study of how workers are meeting family obligations. Until now, no one has known how common it is for working Americans to need to interrupt their work schedules to care for a child, grandchild, niece, nephew, parent, grandparent, aunt, or uncle. Although people have known how commonly their own work was being interrupted, they have not been able to measure their families' needs against those of most other Americans. Employees have learned to keep quiet about their family needs. Sadly, they have learned that saying they have to leave the office for a meeting or for their own medical appointments is far more acceptable than saying they have to leave to take a child to the doctor or to visit an elderly relative in the hospital, which might lead their employers to question their work commitment.[15] As a result, employees often do not know how frequently their coworkers are interrupting their work to meet family needs—nor do most employers or supervisors.

To determine the extent of predictable and unpredictable interruptions, we spoke with the Daily Diaries Study participants every day for an entire week. Each day, they told us whether they had to interrupt what they were doing, cut back their work time, or leave work altogether to meet the needs of family members. They told us whom they were caring for and what kind of problems arose. Their stories and the statistics that came out of this study are the focus of Chapter 2. If you are familiar with the problems of most families, go first to the chapters about the effect on children and about inequalities.

Data on work disruptions indicate how both employers and working adults are being affected by our nation's failure to address working families' needs. In Chapter 3, I examine the stark impact of outdated working conditions and inadequate social supports on children's welfare. Although my own and others' research has shown that having parents available and involved in the care of children with acute and chronic health conditions is vital, our studies showed that many parents lacked paid leave and that those who received no paid sick or vacation leave often had to let their sick children stay home alone, had to entrust them to the piecemeal care of others, or had to send them to school ill. My research team talked with child-care providers and teachers who were struggling to meet the needs of sick and healthy children simultaneously. While some parents told us about having to deal with hospitalizations that became necessary after they had felt compelled to send their sick children to day care or school, others told us about losing jobs because they took time off to care for their sick children. The problems they faced are described in Chapter 3.

Chapter 3 also details the impact of parental working conditions on children's education in America. One of the most important determinants of how children fare in school is parental involvement. My research unit conducted some of the first studies to examine whether parents' working conditions allowed them to meet with teachers and learning specialists and to address the crises that arose in their children's education. Our research also examined how often parents of school-age children had to work in the evening or at night, when their children needed them most. We focused on several issues, including what happens when adequate care is not available for school-age children during evening hours. We found that when parents had to work evening shifts regularly—as has become increasingly necessary in the twenty-four-hour economy of the United States—their children were more likely to be faring poorly in math and more likely to fail in school. And when parents had to work night shifts regularly, their children were more likely to get in trouble and to be suspended from school. Many parents—often those with the least seniority and the youngest children—faced a choice between no job and an evening or night job, whether or not any services were available for their children and other dependents during those hours.

If it is not work itself but the combination of poor working conditions and next to no social supports that is affecting too many of our children in general, what does it mean to children with special needs? In Chapter 4, I present the results of research in which we interviewed working parents of children with special health and developmental needs. When working conditions are poor, when community-based services for working families are inadequate, and when public policy has failed to address the dramatic change in the nature and conditions of parents' work, children with special needs suffer first: Their more frequent health problems mean their parents are in greater need of paid leave from work. The greater difficulties they face at school mean their parents are in greater need of the leave time or flexibility at work that allows them to meet with learning specialists and of work schedules that enable them to assist with homework. Those from low-income families suffer even more because income limitations further restrict the options for the added care these children need. How well we as a society meet the needs of these families is a sign of much more than a readiness to address "special needs." It is a prime indicator of our ability and willingness to meet the health and developmental needs of *all* children.

Many working parents who are struggling to ensure adequate care for their children are also trying to meet the needs of their elderly relatives. We as a nation have barely begun to address the fact that over the same period in which the nature of work was transformed, the demographics of families changed substantially: Whereas 3 percent of Americans were age 65 or older in 1870, 13 percent were that age at the end of the twentieth century.[16] Public attention to this transformation has focused on whether Social Security will face a financial deficit rather than on what the combination of women's and men's increased labor force participation, coupled with the simultaneous increase in elderly people's needs for assistance, will mean for a caregiving deficit. In Chapter 5, I frame the debate about caregiving and the aging of America in facts gleaned from our study of more than two thousand working adults aged 25 to 74 who were asked how much time they spent providing care to their children and parents, as well as how much time they spent receiving care from their children and parents. My research team analyzed the data to learn how many working adults could count on their own parents to help with their children, whether the adults' parents were helping occasionally or for many hours a month, how many working parents were caring for both their own parents and their own children, and how the caretaking arrangements were affecting the lives of all three generations. In Chapter 5, I also look beyond the false dichotomy currently common in discussions about older Americans and caregiving: namely, the assumption that every older American needs assistance against the assumption that they all are willing and able to care for the nation's children.

Whether the issue is elder care or child care, the experiences of low-income families are sounding early, grim warnings for the nation as a whole. When local communities and state and federal governments fail to provide essential services, families who have more money can sometimes partially or temporarily fill the gaps themselves. While middle-class families may not be able to afford the full-time care a disabled parent needs, they may still be able to afford to have someone check on that parent during the day, whereas a family living in poverty could not. While lack of availability of high-quality after-school care may make it impossible for all families to find the care their school-age children need, the higher income of a middle-class family may enable them to at least find a baby-sitter so that a child is not left home alone. While the threat of job loss or other retribution from employers may prevent professionals from using unpaid leave very often, single parents living in poverty may never be able to afford to take unpaid leave. As a result, when communities do not provide after-school care, poor children are the first ones to be left on their own. When communities do not provide elder care, the elderly poor are the first ones to fail to receive essential services that may determine whether they eat three meals a day. While poor families face risks sooner, their experiences say a great deal about the gaps in services that all families across the country face.

Despite the higher risks low-income working families face, strikingly little attention has been paid to their experiences. For decades, most of the work-family literature has focused on middle- and upper-class families' experiences, partly because the research base has been limited and partly because newspaper, magazine, and book publishers were unwilling to print many stories about the poor. Given the relative dearth of writing and information about the experiences of working-poor families, perhaps it should not come as a surprise that current public policy debates resemble pulp fiction. In Chapter 6, I discuss the results of a series of national studies I am leading on how the conditions faced by working-poor families compare to those faced by other working families in America. We are finding that on nearly every measure, working-poor families are facing significantly worse conditions than others. Poor wages are critical to family welfare, but their impact is exacerbated because these workers also receive less paid sick leave and less paid vacation leave, have less flexibility, and have little or no voice in selecting their work schedules. These and other working conditions substantially limit poor families' ability to meet the needs of dependent children, elderly parents, and disabled family members—and thereby dictate the chances of success not only of working adults but of their children and other dependents.

Families living in or near poverty are not the only ones paying a disproportionately high price. Like the poor, women face both a higher caretaking burden and worse working conditions. In Chapter 7, I present the results from our various national studies on the conditions that working women face. I show that, ironically, while working women are disproportionately responsible for caring for children, the elderly, and disabled adults, they face significantly greater work-related barriers to providing that care than do men. Among other disadvantages, women are less likely than men to receive paid sick leave that they can take to care for children, to be able to adjust their starting or quitting times to care for family members, or to have any latitude in deciding how they get their work done. Together, women's higher caretaking burden and the barriers to caregiving while working constrain their ability to succeed at work and limit their ability to care for family members. Chapter 7 demonstrates how in the case of gender, as in the case of class, America's failure to adapt workplaces and social institutions to the needs of working families is leading to an exacerbation of the inequalities that exist in our nation.

In Chapter 8, the conclusion, I focus on what must be done differently to meet the caregiving needs of our country. Until now, the United States, more than any other nation, has left it to corporations to handle the question of whether children with health problems, children whose parents must work evenings, and elderly Americans in need of basic care will receive the assistance they need. But corporations do not see addressing these issues as their primary or even their secondary business, and the majority of corporations have not voluntarily provided paid family leave or other necessary benefits. We must begin by recognizing that this laissez-faire approach to the needs of working families—an approach unique to the United States—has failed. The United States lags behind the more than 120 countries around the world—ranging from France to Tanzania, from Japan to Brazil, from Indonesia to Sweden—that provide paid maternity leave. The other countries have in common neither political form nor government size. What they share is a commitment. In Chapter 8, I examine how and why the U.S. corporate approach differs from theirs, as well as why a purely corporate solution to providing quality care for infants and preschoolers, after-school care for older children, or home assistance for older people is unrealistic and inadequate.

What is essential? Our nation must make a commitment to address the daily care needs of all Americans—including ensuring that all children receive the care and education they need and that adults receive care when they need it—not only to support working families but also to advance the precepts of equal opportunity and equal access. Furthermore, we must guarantee a safety net for working Americans when urgent needs arise, one that includes paid leave and flexibility so that workers can care for sick family members, address urgent child- and elder-care needs, and meet with their children's teachers to address important educational issues. Chapter 8 discusses these and other components of solutions to the widening gap between caretaking demands and resources.

What is the price of doing nothing? A very high one, according to the findings from both the national and the urban studies I have conducted: The inequalities that already exist across the social divides of class, gender, and disability will become more pronounced. But the findings of these studies make it equally clear that America's failure to address the needs of working families affects *all* of us—all ages, races, classes, family structures, and genders. The solutions we develop need to be universally available—equally available to men and women, for example, and equally available to those with low and middle incomes. They should be designed to benefit families in which one adult stays at home as well as those families in which all adults are engaged in wage or salary work. Developing comprehensive, fair, universally available solutions is in fact essential to the fate of our country.

CHAPTER TWO

Predictably Unpredictable:
The Lives of Working Americans

THE FIRST TIME we interviewed Karin Arnette, she was standing outside her front door, watching, as she explained, for someone who looked lost. When we returned, Karin was inside. Mason, one of her 11-year-old twins, lay in bed in the next room because of an asthma exacerbation brought on by a recent bout of the flu. Had he not been sick, Karin would have been at work at the hospital. Although scheduled for only thirty hours a week, she was working forty hours because her family needed the money.

Karin was one of the more than one hundred parents of whom we conducted in-depth interviews in the Urban Working Families Study and one of the more than 7,500 working Americans interviewed for the studies in this book. Her story is told here because it is representative of the problems working Americans face as they try to look after their families, meet routine needs, and address unexpected problems—whether they develop because a child is sick or an elderly parent needs help eating. Warm and welcoming, at each meeting Karin invited the interviewer into her small, neat living room, where framed photographs of her four children were displayed and toys lay in view. Besides the toys, there was a computer in the living room with educational software. Karin did everything she could for her children's education. She expressed deep pride in the fact that her oldest daughter, Heather, had just finished college, when Karin had never had a chance to attend.

Neither Karin nor her husband, Carl, gave up easily on anything. Both had been willing to work long hours and difficult schedules to provide as best they could for their family. Since their first child's birth, Carl had had a full-time job working for the city. After Tricia was born, Karin worked part-time during the day to make ends meet and left Tricia with a baby-sitter. But Karin described discovering that the baby-sitter she could afford was neglecting Tricia, then less than a year old: "One day I came and I asked her to watch [Tricia] and I left her. But when I came back, [the baby-sitter] had gone back to sleep. The lady had my daughter on this mattress with no sheets." While the baby-sitter slept, the infant was left alone with no one to watch her.

Unable to find or afford better child-care arrangements, Karin switched to evening work and cared for the children during the day. The whole family had dinner together after Carl got home from work. With everyone together, dinner was a brief respite when they could tell each other about what had happened during the previous day and plan for the next. Then Carl cared for their children while Karin worked from seven to eleven at night. Although Karin and Carl saw little of each other, the schedule was better than leaving their daughter in the dangerous child-care settings they could find and afford. One of their early baby-sitters, after drinking at night, had a hard time even coming to the door in the morning.

Juggling day and evening shifts worked until Karin gave birth to twins. Then Karin's part-time wages combined with Carl's weren't enough to make ends meet anymore. Carl began working a second job three evenings a week, and Karin switched to working a full night shift. With Carl working days and evenings and Karin working nights, there was always a parent available. But it meant that after spending each night walking, standing, and completing patient's charts, Karin had to come home and care for her young children all day. "Nights. I hated [working] nights," she recalled. "I couldn't really get a good sleep [ever]." During three years on the night shift, she barely slept, and she dragged herself through both the days and the nights. Karin described that period as "like a nightmare":

> I always wanted to try to catch some sleep so I could get there the next day. I just couldn't even think. It just clogged my memory and everything. It really did a job on me and I haven't been right since. ...It is just not good if you have kids at their age. I just couldn't spend any valuable time with them. I was always just sleepy or cranky. "Hurry up because I gotta get some sleep and I gotta go to work."

While she was working the night shift, arthritis set in. Her physician told her she had to switch back to the day shift for her health, but months passed before her supervisor would allow her to stop working nights.

The routine is different now on the day shift, with her youngest children in school. Now she at least has a chance to sleep. Each morning, Karin gets her children ready for school and takes them there, and then she goes to work. After returning from work, she helps them with homework. With Carl working two jobs to make ends meet, Karin does most of the child care and household work alone. Mason's asthma requires daily attention, and Karin must ensure that he regularly gets his inhaled medicine to help stave off the worst exacerbations and hospitalizations. Mason's twin sister, Andrea, who has a learning disability, also needs extra help. Speaking of times she doesn't help Andrea immediately, Karin says, "She'll sit there. She'll hold this paper until I actually sit down and sit with her and work with her." But while doing her homework, Andrea gets angry—at herself, at the learning disability, and at whomever is trying to help her. Karin struggles to give Andrea the help she needs without shortchanging the other children.

Managing the customary day-to-day care of their children—in the absence of affordable, high-quality preschool and school-age child care—was only one part of the problem for the Arnettes. As with most other families, taking care of children and adult family members' sporadic needs disrupted work schedules. While some of the interruptions were predictable, others were utterly unpredictable. The children needed to see doctors for routine care. Karin also had meetings with her children's teachers. Andrea and Mason each had four grading periods, and all parents were asked to meet with teachers during two of the four to discuss how their children were faring in school. There were school breakfasts three times a year when parents were expected to learn about what was going on in the classroom so they could better help their children. Nothing could have been more reasonable or important than the combined half-dozen school meetings. However, Karin and Carl, like the majority of American parents, found that neither public policies developed by governments nor private policies formulated by employers allowed them to visit their children's school.

The Arnettes faced additional challenges. Mason and Andrea both received speech therapy, and Andrea had tutoring for learning disabilities. (One in nine American children have received special education.) To receive these services in the public schools, both children needed federally mandated "individual education plans." For such plans to be initiated and then renewed, Karin or Carl had to go to the school each year and meet with teachers, learning specialists, and principals about their children's progress and future tutoring needs. The meetings make sense; there aren't too many of them. If anything, there are too few for parents to know what's going on in special education and what concerns and insights teachers and tutors have, and for children with learning disabilities to get the help they need.

Karin and Carl needed either to schedule the doctor appointments and the meetings with teachers and learning specialists at a time when they were not at work or to miss work. Whether or not to miss work was usually not their choice. The scheduling depended, instead, on the availability of doctors and the schedules of teachers, tutors, and principals. Occasionally, teachers held evening meetings and clinics had evening hours.

Because Karin was lucky enough to receive paid vacation leave, she could plan some of the meetings then. But she used most of her paid leave to cover a fraction of the days when her children had no school —snow days, teacher-training days, holidays, and school vacations. Karin stayed with her job because it allowed some flexibility to meet family demands. She reflected, "Sometimes I think about leaving and switching, but then I say, Well, these hours are flexible. ...Instead of starting over fresh from the bottom someplace else, I just stay there even—though in my department, there's not really much chance for advancement. But I just kind of put that aside."

No planning could be done, though, for the unpredictable demands that all families face, such as illness. When both Karin and Carl were working day shifts, one of them had to find some way of caring for a sick child. The twins had frequent ear infections and the associated high fevers—among the most common acute illnesses preschool children experience. Their school—like most other schools and child-care centers across the country—would not let children with fevers attend, because the staff could not readily determine whether or not the fevers were due to a contagious disease that would rapidly spread to all the other children. Even when their school knew the fever was due to an infection already being treated with antibiotics, they were inadequately staffed to care for children who required additional attention.

Karin and Carl also had to deal with Mason's asthma, a chronic and recurrently acute condition that required close attention many times each year when the breathing difficulties worsened. Their challenges mirrored those of many other parents, since asthma is the most common chronic health condition among children in the United States, and nearly one in ten children has asthma or reactive airway disease. Over the years, both Karin and Carl had come to recognize the signs that led to the emergency room visits: Mason's neck would sink in, his chest would be sucked back toward his backbone, and his nose would flare as he struggled to breathe. When Mason was barely able to breathe and had to be hospitalized, Karin would take time off from work to be with him. Her supervisor at work said, "Okay, we understand, but we depend on you here." She replied, "Well, I'm sorry, but that's my son and the bottom line is my son needs me. If I have to lose the job, I'll lose the job because at least I have my son."

Karin described one episode while she was on the night shift:

> Mason was so sick, and he was in the hospital because of his asthma. He was little, and they were coming in sticking him every minute and doing these treatments. I had to be there with him. I'd other kids at home, so my husband was home with the kids. I was there with Mason and [my supervisor] was just like, "Isn't there someone else that can do it?" I'm like, "The bottom line is, I'm his parent and that's where I'm going to be. I got to be there for him. Even though I need the job, that's why I'm here."

Karin explained that she "usually stayed home with him when he was sick with his asthma just to make sure he was over everything. Sometimes he'd have to take the medicine for five days and then taper off." (I readily understood her caution, for I had interviewed other parents who had sent children with asthma exacerbations to child care or school, only to have picked them up later in severe respiratory distress and requiring emergency care.)

Karin noted that between Mason's first and seventh birthday,

I missed a lot of work, took a lot of time off from work when he was sick because he'd end up in the hospital. ...They would always keep him overnight and then the next day [say,] "We'd like to keep him another night." And then he'd end up staying three days at least in the hospital. Then I'd have to stay with him. So [those were] tough years when he was younger when he was sick.

Recently, his asthma had appeared to improve, and aggressive medical treatment including steroids had reduced the hospitalizations. But the apparent remission had not proved permanent. "We thought he was growing out of his asthma," she said. "Then, right after [the children] had the flu shot ... he got this ... awful cold ... just seemed like it triggered something." He was close enough to the edge that a simple cold following a flu shot could push him over.

The social dialogue about caretaking responsibilities often sounds as if they end when children reach adolescence. But this is far from the reality. For the Arnette family, as for millions of working Americans, problems arose in how to care for their school-age and adult children, disabled family members, and elderly parents as well as for their children when they were young. Just as problems arose that required Karin and Carl to help their school-age twins, so too were there times when their adult daughter needed them. While pregnant with her first child, Heather became sick and was hospitalized for three weeks. Karin used every lunch hour and break she had to visit her daughter in the hospital. She felt lucky that the hospital was near enough to her workplace that she could visit during the day without missing work. Then Karin's mother had to be hospitalized at the same time because a foot infection had spread through her blood and become a serious systemic infection. Placed on intravenous antibiotics, she had to stay in the hospital for six weeks. In the morning, with her adult daughter and her mother both hospitalized, Karin would get her younger children dressed and fed, take them to school, and then go to work. She would spend her break visiting Heather. At the end of work, she would make dinner for her other children and take them to visit her mother. Karin was able to keep her job, but she spent every spare waking moment caring for her family members. At night, she would leave home to pick up her husband from work. Although her entire attention was devoted to her family, Karin felt guilty about not being able to do enough for any one person. "I just felt so bad. I felt like I had to be there for everybody."

When she had taken leave time over the years to care for family members, Karin had been penalized at work. The consequences were not always immediate, although at times, severe critiques from her supervisor were. At other times, little would be said until a yearly evaluation occurred. "When it was time for an evaluation or a raise or something like that, they would say, 'Well, you missed so many days.'" At those times, said Karin, "they punish you a little for your kid being sick and wanting to be a good parent and stay home and take care of them." She was more fortunate than other parents we interviewed who lost their jobs as a result of days taken to care for sick or hospitalized children.

Of the period when both her mother and her daughter were in the hospital, Karin said, "I felt really overwhelmed. I felt sad a lot." She took no time off from work because she felt she had no other choice. In the end, instead of her work taking the hit, her health did. Her arthritis flared worse than it ever had, in spite of her multiple medications. "The pain [from the arthritis worsening] didn't actually start coming until after [they were in the hospital]. It was almost like it just held on and held on. Once it was over, everything just went crazy." Forty years old at that time, she described her body as like that of a 60-year-old woman. When we interviewed Karin, the smooth skin on her face when she was at rest made her look relatively youthful. But Karin's face wrinkled in concentration and pain from severe arthritis when she made even simple movements such as picking up the mail. The arthritis slowed her walking and, even more so, bending. In the end, she had no choice but to go on a month of temporary disability leave from work.

Karin Arnette's experiences with absences and family work disruptions are important to retell because they represent the experiences of many other families in the United States. Karin had unpredictable absences because her children became sick with common problems: during the course of a year, American children experience 94 million episodes of respiratory illness and 19 million acute ear infections.[1] Like Karin's children with special educational needs, more than 3 million other schoolchildren in the United States have a learning disability. The problems Karin's mother experienced are similarly widespread; one in six Americans 65 years old or older who is not living in an institution has difficulty meeting basic care needs.[2] The demands and needs Karin and Carl struggled with were unique and yet at the same time were playing out in various ways for millions of other American families.

The National Picture

To find out how common the Arnette family's experiences with work and family are, we interviewed a representative sample of 870 adults living across the United States and spoke with each one every day for a week about working while caring for family members. What follows is their story—the story of a week in the life of America. In listening carefully to these people, we were struck by four things: how many Americans are affected, how often caregiving and work responsibilities conflict, how wide a range of family members must be cared for, and how many different caretaking responsibilities working Americans must meet.

Only a small fraction of the problems working families told us about were covered by the Family and Medical Leave Act (FMLA). Passed by Congress in 1993, the FMLA is the only federal policy that addresses the need for adults to take leave from work to care for family members; it requires employers to provide up to twelve weeks of unpaid leave to care for a child, parent, or spouse. However, the FMLA covers only half of all working adults: those who work in firms that employ fifty or more people and who have worked at least twelve months and for at least 1,250 hours in the prior year for their current employer. In addition, the FMLA only covers births, adoptions, and major illnesses. While health-related problems were the most common reason employees in our study took leave to help family members, they accounted for only 29 percent of work-related absences. Furthermore, most children's illnesses requiring parental absence from work would not have qualified under the FMLA as major illnesses. Family members' needs in our study were far more varied and complicated than those covered by the FMLA. Twenty-two percent of cutbacks were taken to address problems with child care, 5 percent to provide for elder care, 3 percent to address children's school needs, 10 percent to provide transportation to family members, 16 percent to provide other instrumental support, 3 percent to cope with a death, 1 percent to deal with divorce, and 15 percent to provide emotional or other support (see Figure 2.1).

Work schedules are based on the assumption that employees will contribute in an uninterrupted way, but the demands placed on individuals by family and friends are neither predictable nor confined to nonworking periods. During the interview week, 30 percent of the respondents had to cut back on at least one day to meet the needs of family members, 12 percent needed to cut back on two or more days, and 5 percent needed to cut back on three or more days. While all of the working adults aged 25 to 74 had significant caretaking responsibilities, those aged 35 to 44 were shouldering the greatest amount of caretaking.

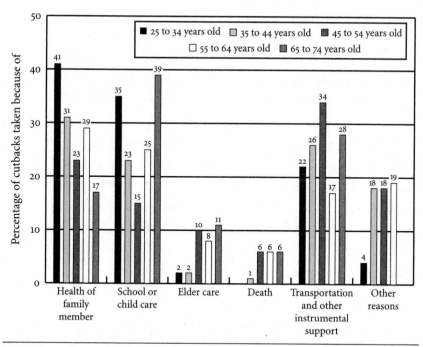

FIGURE 2.1   Respondents' Reasons For Taking Cutbacks (by age of respondent)

NOTE: The figure is based on data we collected in the Daily Diaries Study. (As some residents took cutbacks for multiple reasons, responses may total more than one hundred.)

In that age group, 35 percent had to cut back on at least one day a week to meet the needs of family members, compared to 27 percent of those aged 25 to 34, 29 percent of those 45 to 54, 28 percent of those 55 to 64, and 25 percent of those 65 to 74. Women were more likely to take cutbacks than men, but men still had a large number of cutbacks to meet the needs of family members. Thirty-five percent of the women and 24 percent of the men had to cut back on at least one day in seven.

Extent of Caregiving

The focus of work-family debates over the past two decades and of private- and public-sector policies has been on young parents caring for infants and preschoolers. This is an important piece of the work-family pie, but it is only one small piece, as shown clearly in our interviews. When we asked people about work disruptions associated with care for family members, every age group clearly had sizable caregiving responsibilities. What was different from group to group was who was being cared for. Younger adults were more frequently caring for children, and the middle-aged were more often caring for their parents. In addition, as they aged, the working Americans we talked with were more likely to be caring for their spouses and partners as well as their grandchildren. The full circle of individual and family life courses intersected—and often conflicted—with work demands over and over.

Employees' children accounted for more cutbacks than any other group receiving care, but even when adult children were included as

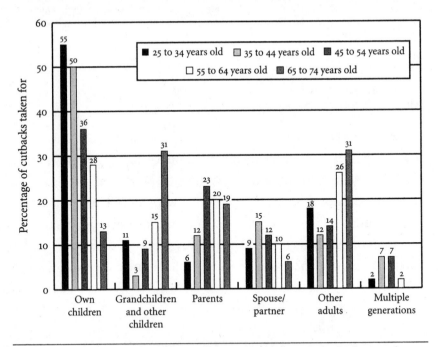

FIGURE 2.2   People Being Cared For by Respondents Taking Cutbacks (by age of respondent)

NOTE: The figure is based on data we collected in the Daily Diaries Study.

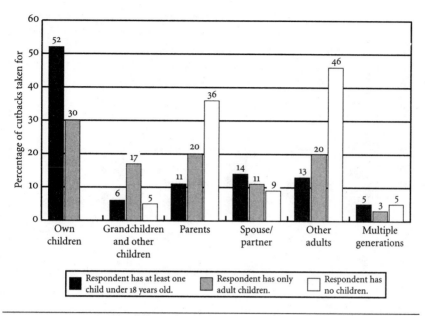

FIGURE 2.3 People Being Cared For by Respondents Taking Cutbacks (by presence and age of children)

NOTE: The figure is based on data we collected in the Daily Diaries Study.

well as preschool and school-age children and even when health and educational needs were included as well as child-care and other needs, they still accounted for only 42 percent of cutbacks. Fifteen percent of cutbacks were taken to care for parents, 12 percent for spouses or partners, 7 percent for grandchildren, and 24 percent for other family members.

Respondents aged 25 to 34 were more likely to be taking cutbacks for their own children; and those between 65 and 74, for grandchildren (see Figure 2.2). People in our study who had no children of their own took cutbacks for other children, such as nieces and nephews, and were the most likely to take cutbacks for parents and other adults (see Figure 2.3). While women were somewhat more likely to have taken cutbacks to care for children and parents, men were more likely to have done so to help spouses or partners (see Figure 2.4).

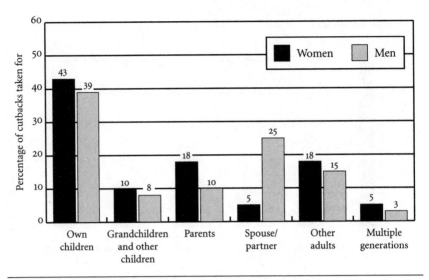

FIGURE 2.4   People Being Cared For by Respondents Taking Cutbacks (by gender of respondent)

NOTE: The figure is based on data we collected in the Daily Diaries Study.

Caring for Children

Many of the people we interviewed spoke of child-care problems like those Karin Arnette faced. As with Karin, many were in jeopardy when they could not afford reliable child care. Respondents living at or below 125 percent of the federal poverty level were more likely to take cutbacks for child-care reasons. Thirty-three percent of the cutbacks taken by low-income respondents were for child care, compared to 21 percent for middle- and higher-income respondents. People in low-skill jobs also had to deal with inflexible schedules that limited their options at work and complicated their responsibilities at home. Still, those with better work situations and higher income levels also struggled to juggle their child-care, work, and household-care responsibilities. Desiree Rogers had two daughters: one 11 years old, the other 7 years old. She worked full-time year round as an office supervisor. Her husband worked ten-hour days as a truck driver. During the week we interviewed her, Desiree had to cut back on two days. She missed work so she could take her younger daughter to the doctor. She also had to take two hours off from work so that her older daughter could get the hepatitis vaccine she needed before entering seventh grade.

While the needs of children clearly change with age, the fact that providing them with effective support takes time away from work does not change. The 870 families we interviewed for a week made that fact clear, as well as their strong commitment to their children. Kelley Hennessy, who was divorced, had four children, ages 15 to 21. She worked as an auditor at a day job forty-five hours a week and at an evening and weekend job another twenty hours. She worked evenings four times a week, as well as weekends two to three times a month. Providing care for her teenagers was stressful, and the stress at home frequently made her irritable at work. In turn, the fatigue and pressure from work affected the attention she gave at home. Kelley had few supports and seldom had real conversations with her neighbors, but she could occasionally rely on family or friends for help. When her teenage daughter had a bad stomach flu, there was no one to help. During the week we interviewed her, Kelley needed to take time off from work to see that her daughter got enough fluids.

Lois Flavin, a married mother of four, worked from eight in the morning until five in the evening as an adjuster; her commute added an hour to each end of the workday. Despite this schedule, she was largely responsible for the household chores, which took twenty hours a week. Her work situation was worse than it had been in the past. Lois was also having problems with her marriage. Although her husband had increased the hours he worked as an engineer to cover more of their child-rearing costs, they still had financial problems. Caring for their daughters, ages 10 to 19, fell largely on Lois's shoulders. Over the course of three months, she had had to reduce her work time on four days to care for her children; her husband had not cut back at all. During the week of the interviews, one of her daughters had needed to see the doctor; Lois was the one who had to leave work three hours early to take her.

Through our interviews, we found that in two-parent families, mothers continue to bear more responsibility for children than do fathers. This was Edie Bernard's experience, just as it was the biography of Desiree Rogers, Lois Flavin, and Karin Arnette. At 37, Edie Bernard had health problems that limited her ability to walk more than several blocks at a time, bend, kneel, or do any vigorous activity. Stress at work frequently made her irritable at home, and she felt her chances of keeping her job for the next two years were poor. Edie explained that she spent forty hours per week doing household chores, while her husband did none. During our interview week, Edie said, "I had to leave work for three hours to deal with the dentist appointment [for her two children, ages 8 and 11]. ...I do price changes—I have to print out the sheets and do the price changes. I got zip done today. Means I'll have to work twice as hard tomorrow." Edie showed many signs of depression: She said she had been sad for more than two weeks in a row, had lost interest in much of life, had trouble concentrating, and felt worthless and tired.

Most of the reasons parents needed to take leave from work to help school-age children were covered neither by the FMLA nor by existing programs serving school-age children. Leroy Stewart explained, "The school decided not to have school for children, but they decided to have school for teachers [and their training]. ...We spent a lot of time trying to figure out what we're going to do for tomorrow. ...I'll either have to take time off or leave work early in order to be back here with the kids." Leroy and his wife, who each worked forty hours a week, did not want to leave their 6- and 9-year-old children home alone. They, like many other parents such as the Arnettes, had great difficulty finding child care throughout the school year, especially when school policies resulted in sporadic days off for the children.

Many parents also have to cope with school bus schedules that can take children home at two or three in the afternoon but do not provide transportation at the end of after-school activities or studies. Bob Dorman had to leave work to pick up his daughter from high school and take her home because she had stayed late to do work for one of her classes and there was no bus for her to take after that. Bob was fortunate to have enough flexibility in his marketing job to be able to take time off from work when his daughter needed to stay late for academics. Like the school closings for teacher development days, the bus schedules reflected a school system unresponsive to the needs of working families. They led to needless work disruptions—ones caused by outdated social structures that are penalizing children, working adults, and employers alike.

Caring for Parents

Among our respondents, cutbacks to assist with elder care were higher for people 45 or older. For Peter Dunning, both his children and his parents needed his time. A married computer analyst, he left home just after eight in the morning and got back around seven in the evening. In addition, he had to work two to three nights a week and most weekends. Work was stressful not just because of the hours but because of interactions with coworkers. Peter had a 17-year-old daughter and a 20-year-old son, both of whom he needed to help with emotional problems and daily issues at school. At the same time, Peter's father was suffering from heart disease. Peter cut back multiple times during the week we interviewed him. First, he left work to visit his father after open-heart surgery. Three days later, he explained, "My father had a cardiac arrest while recovering from open-heart surgery last night. I found out about it this morning. I left work after three hours, and I've been down at the hospital ever since then."

In the case of serious family illnesses, the question is, what happens to the Americans whose jobs are not covered by the FMLA or who cannot afford unpaid leave while caring for their families? Robin Berland reported,

> My mother is terminally ill. News came in this morning that we're not giving her food because they're afraid she will swallow it down the air passage and she'll develop pneumonia. So we're not giving her food and we're not giving her any of her regular pills. She's at the stage where we're trying to manage her pain and discomfort with just morphine three times a day and a heavier dose at night. So my entire schedule was spent down there. She lives about 150 miles away.

Robin worked fifty-five hours a week, fifty-one weeks a year, some evenings and weekends, just to earn $29,000. She had breast cancer herself.

For other families, daily care needs of disabled parents and spouses disrupted work as much as sudden health problems. Julie Austin, a bank manager and married mother of a 2-year-old son, had thyroid disease, migraines, and skin problems requiring treatment. Her husband worked fewer hours at his job as an administrator than she did, but she provided most of the care for their son, while also caring for her father. She explained during the interview week, "I'm moving my father up here from Texas. He had a stroke three years ago, and I'm his guardian. I spent about three or four hours [working on the move.] He lives in Texas now in an assisted living facility, and that's what he'll move up to here." Four days later, she had to take off time from work to deal with his health insurance, and more time two days later to find him doctors near where he'd be living. An only child, she was the sole family member who could provide care. She also bore most of the burden of unpaid work in her home, spending twenty-five hours a week doing household chores versus her husband's two.

Caring for Spouses and Partners

Many people we interviewed needed to work while looking after spouses or partners. Allison Olmsted, a 68-year-old who worked in sales and had children aged 48 and 41, was a case in point. With health problems common for her age—bone and joint disease, high blood pressure, and foot troubles—she had difficulty with physical activity herself and didn't think she could walk more than a mile. Still, in the beginning of the interview week she explained, "My husband has been in the hospital for the last eight days," and it was up to her to take care of him while working.

But it wasn't only older Americans who were caring for spouses and partners. Allister Lowe, age 40, needed to take off time from work because his wife, 31, had ongoing health problems. A car mechanic, who left for work before six in the morning, Allister regularly worked a sixty-hour week and often needed to work weekends. His main source of social support was his family, and his wife, a homemaker, provided most of the care for their 7- and 2-year-old daughters, except when she was sick. She was in the hospital the week he was interviewed, so he had to take a full day off from work.

Helping Extended Family

Many working Americans are caring for relatives outside their immediate families, when no one else is available. Neal Canney, for example, who worked as a furnace operator, had seven older sisters and one older brother. While he reported that he saw his family less than once a month, they relied on him. When, during the interview week, his sister's car didn't work, Neal left work two hours early to pick up his nephew who was sick at school.

Janet Meehan, who administered social services, routinely worked sixty-hour weeks. Fatigue from work affected her attention at home. She had close relationships with family and friends, whom she saw several times a week and whom she felt she could rely on a lot for help. Still, the math of reciprocal relationships meant she had to provide help in return. During the interview week, for example, Janet needed to take time off to care for her sister-in-law's children.

Christine Reyes was helping her niece and her mother-in-law at the same time. A mother of two, Christine worked from 7:45 A.M. to 5:00 P.M. each day as a teacher. She explained, "My niece is getting a divorce, and she is moving back in with her grandmother. And my mother-in-law is living in a rather small house, so we are trying to rearrange and move things around." Christine was helping them both at the same time while caring for her adolescent children and undergoing treatment for breast cancer.

Gillian Freeman, age 37, was already experiencing the accelerated aging common among the poor. Because of a blocked coronary artery, she had chest pain when she walked, either uphill or on a level surface, and she had asthma, an ulcer, and migraines. She worked two different jobs to support her family on an annual income of less than $22,000. During the week we spoke with her, she had to take time off from work to care for her grandmother and to take her to a clinic appointment. Helping her grandmother was not, however, covered by the FMLA.

Sometimes commitments to friends who were like family led to work disruptions. Gregory Viner explained that he had taken four hours off from work during that interview week. "I had to go and bring my friend home from the hospital—get her home and set up and do things she needed."

Often the political dialogue about how employees can meet family needs is high on rhetoric but low on rationality. That is certainly evident in two assumptions: first, that extended family, friends, and neighbors are meeting the needs of most working Americans' family members, and second, that family, friends, and neighbors are able to help without missing work themselves. Both assumptions ignore the facts. The same major work pressures that apply to Americans who are caring for their own immediate family members apply equally to those helping extended family, friends, and neighbors provide that care.

Where Does That Leave Us?

Health insurers and policy analysts in the public and private sector have argued that relying on family members for help in a wide variety of situations is cheaper for corporations and governments. Yet the same people have silently neglected the other side of the equation, since they have not made it possible for working families to reliably provide that care. Many workers are not covered by the FMLA, and even those who are and who can afford the unpaid leave are facing a growing number of dilemmas. The illustrations given in this chapter, such as helping brothers and sisters or grandparents, are only some of the many necessities not covered by the FMLA.

As a nation, we have to take care not to abandon the health and basic living needs of adults. We have to ensure that the health and educational needs of all our children can be met. It is not feasible to meet these needs without changes in the workplace, and those changes must take place in practice, not just on paper.

At the same time, the number of potential work disruptions is too great for them all to be addressed by providing for paid leave during the workday. Addressing all needs through the workplace would not only be unaffordable for some employers, but it would create an incentive for managers and supervisors to hire those with the least family responsibilities. If managers disproportionately hired people without children, those without elderly caretaking responsibilities, and those least willing to provide care to their families, then employers could lower their costs. And guaranteeing that no corporation and no non-profit organization will discriminate against mothers or fathers, adults with parents in need of care, or others meeting family members' or friends' needs is impossible. When, as a nation, we've relied on employers to provide health insurance, it has resulted both in health insurance being unaffordable to many small employers and in some employers discriminating against employees with the most costly health-care needs. In fact, the incentive for small employers not to hire or not to provide health coverage to an employee with serious medical problems has been tragically large.

Providing reliable, high-quality, routine care and transportation to preschool children, school-age children, and the elderly is essential and will go a long way toward decreasing work disruptions. Changing how services are provided will further reduce the need for work cutbacks. For example, the mandated immunizations for school-age children that are currently given in doctors' offices and clinics, which require parents to miss work, could easily be given at schools. Teacher training could be conducted without closing schools.

While these and other similar changes would greatly reduce the need for people to cut back on work to care for family members, they will not eliminate that need. No one can adequately take the place of a parent who is caring for a child in the hospital or with serious school problems. No one can adequately take the place of an adult who is helping a seriously ill parent in the hospital or moving into a nursing home. The fact remains that adults will need to be able to take leave from work to provide important care to family members.

To be accessible to all Americans, that leave will need to be paid. As it is, poor families have fewer benefits yet face more work disruptions. In our study, cutbacks in order to care for children's needs were more frequent among low-income families, and the actual need was probably higher than reported, since we measured only those days on which cutbacks were actually made. Days on which respondents needed to take time to address important family issues but could not do so because they lacked paid leave and could not afford unpaid leave were not counted.[3] Disproportionately many low-income school-aged children have no way of staying for academic or other extracurricular opportunities that lack public transportation. They are also the most likely to lack any supervision when school is unexpectedly closed, not because their families do not care but because their parents' working conditions do not provide them with options.

In addition, as we saw in the cases of Karin Arnette and many other women interviewed, working women continue to carry a disproportionate amount of the caretaking burden. Because of this fact, the way in which public and private policies address employees' needs in caring for family members will play an essential role in equal opportunities for women to advance in the workplace. Until the workplace penalties that caregivers face, such as Karin's decreased chances for salary increases or promotions, are reduced, women will continue to be more adversely affected than men, and men who are willing to shoulder more caretaking burdens will be discouraged from doing so.

Adapting both social institutions and workplaces so that working Americans can meet the health, educational, developmental, and basic living needs of their family members is critical to everyone in the country, because everyone at some time will be in need of care. It is not only important to those who receive the care; it is also critical in the efforts to ensure equal opportunity in our country.

CHAPTER THREE

Outdated Working Conditions and Inadequate Social Supports: The Impact on Children

FAMILY PICTURES surrounded Nancy McAllister as we spoke with her in her modest, middle-class living room. Framed school photographs of her two sons, 11-year-old Andrew and 5-year-old Jonathan, and a painted portrait of Nancy with her seven siblings adorned the walls. Her duplex was across the street from a rundown auto shop, but the row of two-family houses where she resided was well kept.

When she began work around 8:30 A.M., Nancy occasionally was five minutes late because of the types of problems many parents face: a child not getting dressed fast enough, a delay when dropping off a child at school or day care, or a traffic jam between the school and her workplace. But one of Nancy's supervisors treated being five minutes late—whatever the reason—the same as missing eight hours of work and wrote up every reproach. Since a certain number of written reproaches could lead to her being fired, Nancy set every clock in her house and in her car early so she wouldn't be late. She even set them early by different amounts so she wouldn't be tempted to recalculate how many minutes she actually had before needing to leave. "That clock. ... [is] an hour early. Kitchen is fifteen minutes. This is forty. Car is ten minutes. Anything to fool me, mess with my head, so I know that I'd be on time. It works. My adrenaline's going."

Nancy's job at the post office enabled her to have vacation and sick leave—two of the benefits unions had fought for in the first half of the twentieth century. She had vacation weeks that she could use to care for her children on some, but not all, of their many school holidays. Nancy also had sick leave and was allowed—in theory, at least—to use a portion of her sick leave days to care for family members.

In practice, though, her supervisor penalized her if she took sick days for family members' care, and the supervisor told her to find someone else to care for her children when they were sick. Because of that, Nancy often just sent her children to school when they were ill. But even that didn't always prevent trouble at work. She explained, "One morning, Andrew didn't want to go [to school sick] and I made him go. Because I made him go, I had to come and get him—school wouldn't let him walk home. If I'd kept him [at home, by himself], I wouldn't have had to leave work." When she left work for an hour to pick Andrew up—at the school's insistence—and to drop him off alone at home, her supervisor criticized her for not getting someone else to transport her son. Nancy was relieved when she got sick at the same time as her children because then she could more easily stay home with them. "Last sickness Jonathan had, I was sick with him, so that worked out perfectly," she explained simply.

For Nancy's children, getting to school too early because the clocks had been all reset and being left home alone sick were lesser problems, however, than the routine neglect resulting from the lack of options for their adequate daily care. Her sons were still young, but the combination of her schedule at work and the children's schedule at school meant that they were left alone either in the morning before school or in the afternoon when school ended.

Nancy often had no control over her work hours. Her supervisor assigned the schedules, and over the course of months, Nancy's schedule was changed frequently—and each change necessitated new child-care arrangements. Nancy described two of the schedules she had worked: "If I go in at 6:30 A.M., I'm not [at home] in the morning." On those days, she had to leave her 11-year-old in charge of waking the 5-year-old and getting him dressed, making sure he was dressed warmly enough for the winter. Andrew often had to walk Jonathan to school through patches of uncleared, icy snow covering the sidewalks.

"If I go at 8:30 in the morning," she explained, "I make sure they get their coats and hats and gloves, because they'll tend not to dress appropriately if you don't make sure they're doing it." But on that schedule, her children were alone in the afternoon; the only available baby-sitter worked at another job two afternoons a week. When her schedule was changed on short notice, Nancy had little or no chance of getting her sons into one of the oversubscribed city after-school programs. In addition, Nancy often worked overtime, either because she needed the money or because her supervisor required it. When Nancy had to be on the job from 6:30 in the morning to 5:00 in the afternoon for six months, she saw her children neither before school nor after.

There was little adult help other than Nancy available to Andrew and Jonathan. They had no grandparents nearby. Their aunts and uncles worked, with the exception of Nancy's brother Sam, who had recently fought for release from a mental hospital, where he'd been for more than four years. Sam had no job and often had time on his hands. When Nancy needed help with her sons and had no other alternative, she asked Sam to pitch in, but it wasn't clear whether helping was good for either Sam or the boys. Nancy was sure that her brother needed family contact and support, but he harbored tremendous anger. Nancy told of Sam's yelling at the boys and getting angry at them for not doing something he'd forgotten to tell them to do in the first place. There was little doubt that the time Sam and his nephews had together would have been better for all three of them if there had been another adult around at the same time for support.

From preschool on, neither Andrew nor Jonathan had had reliable, high-quality care. As a preschooler, Andrew was moved from one baby-sitter to the next every few months. When he entered school, he was often left home alone either before or after school. Nancy described one particular week:

> My boss made me work the six o'clock shift while Andrew was six or seven—maybe seven. I would leave him in the morning, and he got up that week and he was on his own. He was scared. And he got in trouble in school a couple of times that week ... arguing with a teacher, fighting with a classmate. I shouldn't have did what my boss wanted. ...They changed my hours without any notice. ... It didn't work for my son because he couldn't handle being in the house alone at that age.

Sometimes, over the years, Andrew faced dangerous situations. For instance, when he was less than 10 years old and home alone with a friend, they lit a match and dropped it, burned the rug, and were lucky not to end up burned seriously themselves.

When Jonathan reached school age, he was left alone in Andrew's care two days a week. Nancy knew that in practice this meant an electronic game, Sega, was Jonathan's baby-sitter. Even those 11-year-olds who can care for themselves fairly well often are not ready to be thrust into the position of caring alone for younger children. But from a very young age, Andrew had been required to act like an adult. Nancy explained, "Andrew has always been my little man—even when he was 2 or 3, like a little adult. ...He just learned young. It was just me and him for a couple years, so I guess he just learned." Andrew had had no other choice, and the tension of being asked to act as an adult came out in his relationship with Jonathan. First, there was the usual sibling tension, which Nancy described: "He watches out for his brother. He's like a big brother. If you see them coming down the street, sometimes he'll have his arm around [Jonathan]. He's real protective. And other times he'll pick on him to death." But the tensions went beyond the usual fraternal fracases, and the root of the unrest lay in the weight of responsibilities placed on Andrew's shoulders. "Most of the time they get along, but sometimes he hates having a little brother." Nancy described how Andrew would at times hurt Jonathan: "I don't know how bad [Andrew] hurts [Jonathan] when he hurts him. Basically he knows how hard he's hurting him. But sometimes he loses his temper. Not too often, thank God, because I don't know what to do."

Being at home with neither adults nor children his age was exacting a heavy toll on Andrew. Pain echoed in Nancy's description of Andrew: "He doesn't really hang out too much. If I was home, he might. We used to have the backyard gate connected to the other yard. Now we have it nailed [shut] because there's no kids in that yard [and Nancy was worried about the adults]. ...There were times when he probably was alone more than he wanted to be." The repercussions for Andrew especially were evident in school. Nancy heard from "the school ... saying he was acting up. ... He was getting aggravated; things were building up inside of him." Nancy reflected, "He'd get in trouble. I could sense that it was my fault because he just was on his own a little more than he should've been. ... I know it was related to that."

Andrew was bright and talented, as his teachers made clear. When he did his work, he was an A student, but he did not always hand in homework projects he was supposed to have done on his own. He could not study in the afternoon, when he had to care for Jonathan. Because of his academic potential, Andrew was placed in an intensive studies program for talented students in the public school system, but he was rapidly removed from it. Instead of excelling at school, as he had the potential to do, Andrew was ending up in detention.

The toll on Andrew was emotional as well as academic. He was sent to a psychiatrist after he "flipped out" on a teacher. "They thought he couldn't handle his anger," Nancy explained, noting that his anger was an ongoing problem. He also had leg problems that (from Nancy's description) may have been psychosomatic. He had few chances to see friends or to relate to children other than his brother, who was more nervous at school and at home than he should have been for his age and who needed special help with prereading and prewriting skills. Andrew, so much in need of care and adult guidance himself, obviously could not offer his younger brother intensive support.

Nancy was all too aware, in addition, of risks her children faced in their urban environment, and her concern was heightened because they both occasionally roamed around the city unsupervised. "Andrew is more of a wanderer than Jonathan, but they are both wanderers. They're kind of easygoing, and they don't realize the danger." Another boy in the community, Andrew's age, who regularly stayed by himself after school, agreed one day to go with some strangers he had met, and after a manhunt he was found dead at the bottom of a river.

The circumstances Nancy and her children were coping with reflect the gaping holes in public support for American working families. Nancy's situation is illuminating not because it is among the worst but because it shows how bad things can get for employees with more than average benefits from their employers when affordable preschool and out-of-school care is unavailable, when employees have little control over their schedules, and when leave to address family needs is inadequate. While the bickering over who is responsible continues, countless children in the United States, like Nancy's, are suffering the consequences of inadequate social supports and outdated work practices.

Inadequate Social Responses to Children's Needs

The school system in the city where we conducted in-depth interviews of Nancy McAllister and other families was typical of many across the country. There were more school holidays than there were months in the year. Thanksgiving vacation. Winter vacation. February and April vacations. The breaks would have been welcome if working parents had had as many.

The holidays were only the beginning of the days on which families had to find a way to care for their children when school was closed and adults had to work. Nearly every month had an "early release day," when the children were sent home at lunchtime and staff stayed on for meetings. As in most other American cities and towns, the school year was only nine and a half months long, and the school day was less than six hours long—a pattern begun when mandatory education first boomed and the majority of the U.S. population worked on farms.[1] At that time, children went home in the afternoons to help work on homesteads where their parents were working, and children were needed during the summer to supply extra hands to harvest crops. In 2000, fewer than 3 percent of Americans work in farming, forestry, and fishing.[2] Most parents—like Nancy McAllister and the parents profiled in Chapter 2—have full-time year-round work schedules at some phys- ical distance from their homes and their children. Even when parents who are working for pay from their homes are taken into account, the percentage of households where there is a parent at home when chil- dren return from school has plummeted. But few schools have changed.

Lack of out-of-school care does not just affect low-income fami- lies, and the risks of being left alone do not affect only poor children. Twice as many parents would like to have an after-school program available to their children as have one, according to the U.S. Department of Education.[3] And the situation is getting worse, not better. The Government Accounting Office estimates that the demands in some urban areas for out-of-school programs will be four times as great as the supply by the year 2002.[4]

Many of the parents in our studies who were seeking after-school care experienced problems with serious consequences. One parent who worked as a homemaker for the elderly tried to get her son into an after-school program, but he was on the waiting list for a year and a half. Unable to get child care and feeling it was unsafe to leave her 8-year-old son alone, she stopped working. But that decision left her family in poverty. It was only after she left her job that an after-care space finally opened up.

Caroline Hardin, a school social worker employed for thirty hours a week, was another parent who faced a gap in care. As troubling as what happened to her children when they were left alone was the societal response:

> [My children] had about twenty minutes to be here alone until I came home. During that twenty minutes, there was an accident that happened. There's some glass doors that go between here and the living room. They were fooling around together. Cassie tried to lock Troy out, and he pushed against the glass door. There must have been a fissure in the glass or something, but it broke and his arm went right through. He really cut himself. And so, we had talked to them about what to do in an emergency. You know, about calling 911, what neighbor on the street they could go to. And they just dashed out of the house together and ran down to a family that lives a couple of houses down.
>
> [The family] didn't take him to the hospital right away because they ... knew I was on my way home, and they ... felt if they took him to the hospital, that DSS [the Department of Social Services, which investigates cases of child neglect and abuse] might get involved because I hadn't been home. So they wanted to wait until I got home. They sent another kid [to our house] to wait for me and tell me what happened. When I got home,

I was immediately taken over, and I rushed Troy to the hospital. [A doctor from her children's health clinic] was there, and she said, "Well, how did it happen?" And she looked at me and I said, "You know, I really didn't hear exactly what happened. Kids, what did happen exactly?" And she said, "Oh, you weren't there?" And, I said, "No." And she said, "Well, who was with them?" And I said, "They were alone for about ten minutes." "Oh, I'm sorry, but we're going to have to investigate this." And I went nuts.

While as a nation we spend few financial resources ensuring that parental or other care is available for children before school, after school, or during vacations or school closings, we readily spend money on children who have been injured—physically or developmentally—when alone. Parents are blamed—whether or not they could have found an alternative—but our nation is rarely held responsible for its complicity.

While both middle-income and low-income children confront potentially devastating gaps, poor children face the greatest risks. When we interviewed parents living in areas of concentrated poverty, they did not express worry about their children's safety when a parent could be with them or when their children were at school or supervised by other adults. They were worried about what would happen to their children when they were left alone. When asked what concern she had about her son's future, one mother explained, "the same concerns that any mother would have over raising a son in a city. Just that I worry with me working, maybe I'm not going to have these perfect hours." She was worried about not being able to be with him in the after-school hours and about his being left alone. The highest crime rates occur in the poorest neighborhoods during after-school hours, and the parents living in those neighborhoods are the ones who can least afford to pay for after-school care.

Some U.S. public schools—but perilously few—have begun to offer extended-day programs. Hawaii is the only state in which the majority of public schools offer extended-day programs. In every other state, fewer than half of all public schools offer programs for children who have no one home in the middle of the working day. In more than half of the states, no more than one in five schools offered programs during the afternoons in 1998. Even where school-age child care is available, it is often unaffordable. Unlike attending public school, attending after-school programs is not free. In fact, the average yearly cost of child care for 8-year-olds is higher in most states than the tuition at state universities.[5]

While the most common problems occur during afternoon after-school hours, on school vacations, and during school closings, parents who have no choice but to work early or late shifts face problems with both early-morning and evening care for their children. Like Nancy McAllister, Elaine Dossous had to leave for work before her 6-year-old twins went to school. She explained, "I would never ever want them to go [to school] alone at age 6. ...I couldn't think straight if I thought they were just walking alone to the school for breakfast." But she couldn't afford not to work. For a while she relied on the makeshift solution of having teenagers in the neighborhood walk the twins to school. No one teenager could help every day, so two adolescents alternated, which increased the likelihood that whoever's turn it was would forget and no one would come for the young twins. But even this patchwork was falling apart for the Dossous twins. The high school changed its hours, and the teenagers could no longer help. Then Elaine began a search for a child in elementary school who could escort her 6-year-olds.

Among nonstandard shifts, the evening shift is the most common, accounting for 40 percent of all nonstandard work shifts among full-time workers and more than half of those among part-time workers. The remaining nonstandard schedules are divided among night shifts, rotating shifts, and split shifts.[6]

Lisa Jenkins worked evenings as a home health aide because that shift was her only option. She left her 5-year-old at home with her older sister, a teenager. Lisa felt that this stopgap was safe enough when her preschooler was healthy, but she worried about what to do if her younger child got sick at night. She felt that her older daughter would not know how to provide care. What's more, Lisa had no car, and the buses stopped running during the night shift.

Nonweekday schedules are on the rise in both North America and Europe.[7] Parents who do evening work clearly have less time to spend with their school-age children. Whereas a mother or father who works from 9:00 A.M. to 3:00 P.M. may be with a 7-year-old child all the time the child is not in school, the parent who works from 3:00 P.M. to 9:00 P.M. may rarely see the school-age child awake during the week and therefore may be able to offer very limited support for the child's cognitive and social development. In addition, parents who are at work during children's after-school hours may have few options if they seek high-quality alternative care for their children.[8] No national studies have been conducted on the availability of evening care, but various regional studies have indicated that only limited evening care is available. The U.S. Department of Labor examined after-hours care in Idaho, and only 12 out of 160 licensed day-care providers were open at eight in the evening.[9]

Employed mothers with limited formal education are more likely to work nonstandard schedules than employed mothers with more than a high school education. Among the women who have school-age children between ages 5 and 13, more than half work a nonstandard shift, either because they cannot get any other job or because working such a shift is required.[10] Moreover, as welfare reform takes full effect nationally and the overwhelming majority of welfare recipients are required to find work, the number of parents who have little choice but to work evenings is likely to increase significantly.[11] Among 18- to 34-year-old employed women who have children 14 or younger, 12 percent of those with a high school education or less work the evening shift, as do 10 percent of those with more than a high school education.[12] Furthermore, the occupations that are expected to grow the most during the coming decade have unusually high percentages of employees working nonstandard hours.[13] A significant number of these occupations will be filled by low-skilled workers, including cashiers, sales clerks, truck drivers, waiters and waitresses, orderlies and attendants, janitors and cleaners, and food-counter workers.

Lack of Child Care for Preschool and Out-of-School Children

During World War II, government-supported child care centers sprang up temporarily so that large numbers of mothers could enter the labor force and fill the jobs left vacant by men gone to war. Then as now, only higher-income parents could afford to pay for one-on-one home-based child care while they were at work. After World War II, though, federal funding for child care was withdrawn, and working parents suffered a significant setback. Even today, the United States does not have the level of governmental support of preschool child care and early education that many industrialized countries with smaller economies have, such as Belgium, Denmark, Finland, France, and Sweden.[14]

The average price charged for child care for a 1-year-old is higher in every state than the average cost of college tuition at the state's universities. Caring for a 4-year-old in a child-care center is likewise more expensive than paying state university tuition in all states. But poor quality is as great a problem as unaffordability. Thirty-eight states have no requirement that family child-care providers be trained, and thirty-two states have no requirement that teachers in child-care centers be trained. Although studies have repeatedly shown that children fare better socially and cognitively when there are fewer children being cared for by each child-care provider, state laws allow large numbers of preschool children to be cared for by a single provider. Six states allow each preschool child-care provider to watch fourteen or more 3-year-olds at a time, forty-three states allow each provider to care for ten or more 3-year-olds, and forty-six states allow each provider to care for four or more infants at a time.[15]

As grossly inadequate as the public and corporate policies regarding preschool child care are, they are far more developed than the policies addressing the needs of school-age children. Those employers who pride themselves on providing benefit packages that make it possible for working parents to care for their children and their work commonly present their parental leave policies and preschool care provisions as prime examples, while doing little or nothing for school-age children. Since the federal government has done little more, school-age children's needs have been largely ignored. As noted earlier, most schoolchildren lack access to formal care in the afternoons and in summer as well as on holidays, snow days, and other school-closing days.

Only 1 percent solutions for school-age children have even been attempted. In his January 19, 1999, state of the union address, President Bill Clinton proposed funds for after-school programs:

> Working parents also need quality child care. ... I ask Congress to support our plan for tax credits and subsidies for working families, for improved safety quality, for expanded after-school programs. ...We can't just hold students back because the system fails them. So my balanced budget triples the funding for summer school and after-school programs, to keep a million children learning."[16]

At a press briefing the same day, senior Clinton administration officials specified an amount for the proposed funding: $600 million. If spread among all school-age children, $600 million comes to less than $24 a year per child. That amount would cover less than a week of after-school care. The average yearly cost of care for an 8-year-old child is $3,433.[17]

Even if it passed Congress, the $600 million investment in after-school programs would represent less than one-quarter of 1 percent additional public funds placed into elementary and secondary education. During the 1993–1994 school year, $288 billion was spent—$265 billion of that in public funds alone—on elementary and secondary school education. State and local governments, the principal funders of primary and secondary education in the United States, supplied $277 billion of the $305 billion in public funds.[18] Even in comparison to the federal government's $35 billion, an additional $600 million in federal funds, if made available, would represent less than 2 percent of the current federal expenditure.

On March 25, 1999, Representative Michael Castle, a Republican from Delaware, introduced the Afterschool Children's Education Act in the U.S. House of Representatives. The legislation contained far less money than even the limited amount the president had proposed. After stating that "approximately 24 million school-age children are in need of adult supervision while their parents are at work," the act proposed to add $10 million to the Child Care and Development Block Grant Act of 1990—meaning that it would add less than fifty cents per year for each school-age child the bill defined in need. The bill went on to say, "Experts estimate that almost 5 million school-age children spend time without adult supervision during a typical week and that these children are more likely to engage in risky behavior such as drug and alcohol abuse, sexual activity, loitering on street corners, and truancy." Even if focused only on these children, the legislation would add just two dollars per year for each of these children who were alone and at high risk. Two dollars will not change Andrew McAllister's situation. If it passed, the bill would have required states to spend at least 1 percent of their child-care funds on school-age children. A mandated minimum of 1 percent—a gross underestimate of the need—accurately reflects the extent to which school-age children are currently over-looked in work-family policy.

Barriers to Parents' Involvement in Education

One of the most important factors affecting how children fare in school is parental involvement.[19] When parents are involved in their children's education, children achieve more in elementary school, junior high school, and high school.[20] Parental involvement is associated with children's higher achievement in language and mathematics, improved behavior, greater academic persistence, and lower dropout rates.[21]

We looked nationally at whether working parents could take time off from work to meet with teachers, principals, and learning specialists; to visit schools; and to help guide their children through difficult periods. We used national data to examine how often parents had paid leave from work or other forms of flexibility that they might use to address these essential needs. At an even more fundamental level, we looked at whether parents could be available in the evenings to help their school-age children. We examined the conditions faced by all families and paid particular attention to families in which a child scored in the bottom quartile on tests of reading, vocabulary, and math. We also looked at the conditions faced by families in which a child was having even more marked problems, as when a child had to repeat a grade or was suspended from school.

We found that across the country, too many parents lacked the paid leave and flexibility they needed to take time from work to help their children with school problems. Disastrously, those who most needed such benefits had the fewest. Families in which a child was in the bottom quartile in reading or math were significantly more likely to face working conditions that made it difficult or impossible for the parents

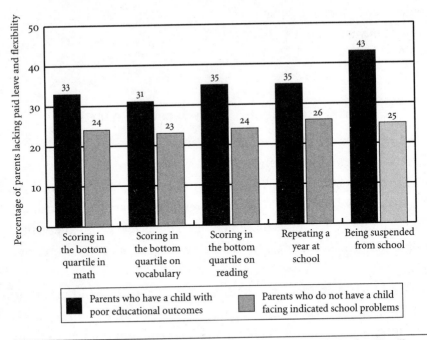

FIGURE 3.1   Poor Working Conditions of Parents of Children at Risk Educationally

NOTE: The figure is based on analyses we conducted with data from the National Longitudinal Survey of Youth. We examined whether parents lacked paid sick leave, paid vacation leave, or scheduling flexibility in their primary job some or all the time between 1990 and 1996. Parents were classified as having paid sick or vacation leave if they reported receiving at least one day of paid sick or vacation leave at their job.

to adequately assist their children. Of parents who had a child scoring in the bottom quartile on math, more than half at times lacked any kind of paid leave, and nearly three-fourths could not consistently rely on flexibility at work. One out of three found themselves at multiple jeopardy, simultaneously lacking paid vacation leave, sick leave, *and* work flexibility (see Figure 3.1). One in six were not able to be available routinely in the evenings because of work, and more than one in ten had to work nights (see Figures 3.2 and 3.3).

Families in which a child scored in the bottom quartile in reading were equally constrained by working conditions. More than half of these parents lacked paid leave, and nearly three out of four lacked

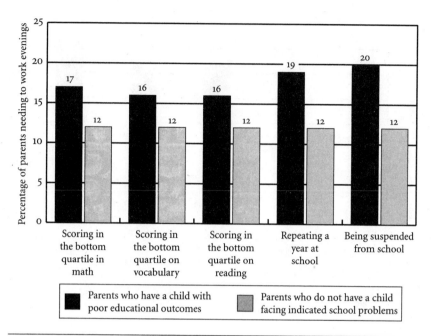

FIGURE 3.2 Evening Work by Parents of Children at Risk Educationally

NOTE: The figure is based on analyses we conducted with data from the National Longitudinal Survey of Youth. Parents needing to work evenings reported working an evening shift at their primary job for some or all of their working years between 1990 and 1996.

flexibility they could rely on. More than one out of three found themselves in one or more jobs between 1990 and 1996 in which they simultaneously lacked paid vacation leave, sick leave, and flexibility (see Figure 3.1). Furthermore, as in the case of the parents of children scoring in the bottom quartile on math, one in six of the parents of children scoring in the bottom quartile in reading worked evenings, and more than one in ten worked some nights (see Figures 3.2 and 3.3).

These potentially ruinous patterns also held for the parents of children who were at greatest risk: those who had to repeat a grade in school or who had been suspended from school. More than half of these parents found themselves at some times lacking any kind of leave they could take to address their children's problems. Four out of ten of

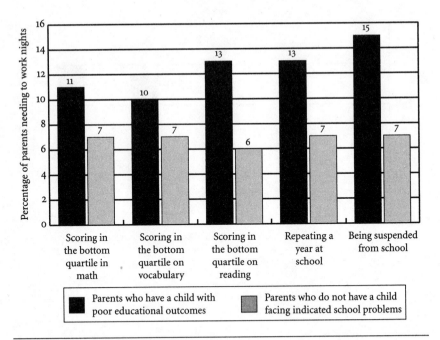

FIGURE 3.3   Night Work by Parents of Children at Risk Educationally

NOTE: The figure is based on analyses we conducted with data from the National Longitudinal Survey of Youth. Parents needing to work nights reported working a night shift at their primary job for some or all of their working years between 1990 and 1996.

these parents found themselves, some or all of the time, in multiple jeopardy (see Figure 3.1). Nearly one out of five of these parents worked evenings, and one out of seven worked nights (see Figures 3.2 and 3.3).

In all these cases, poor parental working conditions disastrously limited the extent to which parents could be available to help children once their education was in trouble. Not having parents available to help in the evenings and nights also appears to have led to children having greater troubles in the first place. Can the relationship between parental working conditions and children's poor school performance be explained by other factors? Even when statistical methods are used to control for differences in family income and in parental education, marital status, and total hours worked, the more hours parents are away from home after school and in the evening, the more likely their children are to test in the bottom quartile on achievement tests (see Appendix C). Similarly, after controlling for other differences, parents who work at night are still 2.7 times as likely to have a child who has been suspended from school.

Barriers to Parents' Involvement in Children's Health Care

Parents have long played an essential role in the health care as well as the education of their children, and many studies over the course of decades have demonstrated the importance of parents' involvement when their children are sick. When their parents are present, sick children have better vital signs and fewer symptoms, and they recover more rapidly from illnesses and injuries.[22] Furthermore, the presence of parents shortens children's hospital stays by 31 percent.[23] Because parental care has proved so important, pediatricians have increasingly offered parents the chance to become involved in different aspects of their children's health care.[24]

Despite the compelling evidence about the value of parents' sharing in their children's health care, little attention has been paid to the factors that influence whether working parents can participate. In the Baltimore Parenthood Study, we asked young parents a series of questions about the factors that enhanced their ability to care for their children who became sick. Parents were asked, among other things, what they did when their children were sick on a regular workday—for example, whether they stayed at home and told those at work that their children were ill, stayed at home and gave a different reason or no reason at all for missing work, or went to work and left their children. Parents who said they stayed at home were asked what made it possible for them to do that—unpaid leave, flexible work hours, working at home, paid leave to care for sick family members, their own paid sick leave, paid vacation or personal days, or other factors.

Fifty-eight percent of parents continued to go to work when their children were sick. Of the 42 percent who were able to stay at home with their sick children, more than half said they could do so because they received some type of paid leave. Twenty-nine percent used paid vacation or personal days, 14 percent used paid leave designed to allow them to care for sick family members, and 11 percent used their own paid sick leave; 11 percent took unpaid leave; and 7 percent used flexible working hours. Twenty-one percent used different work benefits on different occasions. Parents who were single, who were living near or below the poverty level, or who had a high school education or less were significantly less likely to stay at home when their children became sick because they had worse working conditions.

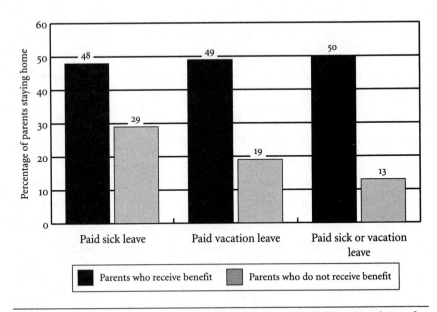

FIGURE 3.4   Percentage of Parents Who Stay Home with Sick Children, by Job Benefit

NOTE: The figure is based on analyses we conducted with data from the Baltimore Parenthood Study.

Our statistical analyses confirmed that the parents who received some type of paid leave were significantly more likely to stay home with their sick children (see Figure 3.4). In fact, the availability of paid leave proved to be the key determinant of the choices made by parents. Those parents who had either sick leave or vacation leave were 5.2 times as likely to care for their sick children as those who did not have such benefits.[25]

In spite of the critical need, the majority of parents do not consistently have paid leave they can use to care for children, and as a result, children are left home alone or sent to school sick. Elisa March, a 33-year-old single mother of one girl, explained in an interview for our Urban Working Families Study, "[My daughter] was sick back in the fall. She got real sick. It was a combination of asthma and just a real bad cold. I remember I had to get in [to work] and so I left her [home]. ...And then I ended up spending almost the whole day at work ... just calling here. ...She needed me here, but I felt like I had to be at work." Eleni Kosnik, a 41-year-old, low-income married mother of two, said she often had to tell one of her sick children, "Here, just take some Tylenol. Just go [to school]." Her response was one we heard many times in the interviews.

Workplace environments influence whether parents can take leave to care for sick family members. Katie O'Donnell, a 26-year-old single mother, was a child-care worker. When her 1-year-old son, Eric, became very sick and had to be hospitalized, she explained,

> I did what I was supposed to do as an employee, and I kept them posted. And he got out of the hospital on Friday morning. And I went to pick up my paycheck so I could go get his prescriptions filled.
>
> And when I walked in there, the person who was in charge of getting a substitute when we were going to be out said, "You gotta be in on Monday." And I said, "I can't let you know yet. He just got out of the hospital. He still has a fever. I can't give that answer now. Sorry, but I can't." And me and her did get into a fight in the office.

But my old supervisor, who was very supportive, went in there right after I came out and said, "How dare you ask her something like that? Her baby just got out of the hospital." ... He had—you name it, he had it: infections, stomach flu, pneumonia.

The majority of child-care providers in our Urban Working Families Study were all-too-familiar with the problem of sick children—from all social classes—being dropped off at school. They generally could tell when parents were dropping off sick children. Kelly Park, a child-care provider at a nonprofit center that cares for children ages 2 months to 5 years, described the typical "Tylenol signs" she often saw—signs that parents had given a feverish child acetaminophen to mask an illness before dropping the child off at the child-care center: "Sometimes, the child tells us that they drank pink medicine at home. When the children are verbal, often they tell us very innocently, 'Oh yes, Mommy gave me medicine at home.' Sometimes you can just tell by their eyes. ...The parent says he's a little tired, and four hours later, after the Tylenol wears off, the fever goes up." We heard a nearly identical scenario from Donna Saffioti, a child-care provider at a private preschool center:

> The children who are older and are able to speak say, 'Oh, I had medicine this morning,' and most of the time, we attributed that to Tylenol. A couple of hours later we check the temperature, and it shoots right up because they had Tylenol at the house to keep the temperature down. ...That goes back to the demands of [the parents'] jobs. It's just hard for them to take time off. ... And so they think maybe we won't catch that, and then the child could be here all day and they wouldn't have to miss work.

Angela Stephenson, a teacher at a preschool child-care center, described another common situation: parents who pretend not to have seen their infants' or toddlers' viral exanthema: "The parents, because they dress the children, it's usually pretty clear from the rash that they should've seen the rash. You can't really miss it, because we change the first diaper at eight-thirty or nine o'clock in the morning, and you see the rash [from the child's being sick] on the stomach or wherever it is. And they just dump that on us."

Sending sick children to child-care contributes to the spread of disease to healthy children and the significantly higher rates of all infectious diseases—particularly respiratory, ear, and gastrointestinal infections—among children attending child-care centers in the United States and other nations.[26] Furthermore, many of the child-care providers we spoke with described having received children whose acute health problems made it impossible to provide adequate care either for them or for the well children under the child-care provider's supervision. Problems arose, for example, because the child-care providers could not keep clean and well hydrated the sick children who were vomiting or had diarrhea, give sufficient attention to the sick children's other needs, and curb the spread of infectious diseases while also trying to care for the healthy children.

The child-care providers' descriptions underscored the amount of one-on-one time and attention needed to meet the basic needs of sick children. Nina Winters, a child-care provider at a public after-school program, described what happened when a child with diarrhea was dropped off. The parent knew the child was sick but did not tell the teacher: "He went to the bathroom in his pants, and we had to clean him up. …The father went off to work knowing his kid was sick. … [The mother] brought him here, and she went to work." Repeatedly cleaning up after a child with diarrhea took the full attention of Winters, who was supposed to be caring for eight to ten other children, too. Angela Stephenson, who works at a private nonprofit center, described parents who brought in children after they were vomiting in the car:

You walk in the door and you can smell the throw-up, and the parents are at the cubby changing the clothes [and] very quickly taking the throw-up ones away. "Oh no, they were coughing and choking in the car. They were eating something in the car. That's all that it is." And then they are sick for the rest of the day.

Obviously, the lack of appropriate care for sick children affects many children, parents, and teachers. Overall, 41 percent of the parents we interviewed extensively in the Urban Working Families Study said their working conditions had negatively affected their children's health in ways that ranged from children being unable to make needed doctors' appointments to children receiving inadequate early care, which resulted in their condition worsening. Even though parents recognized these problems, many knew that if they took time off from work to meet their children's health needs, they would lose essential pay and possibly their jobs. Often parents felt they had little choice but to gamble by either sending their children to child care or school sick or leaving them home alone. Sometimes the gamble led to serious problems. Colleen Brown, a 49-year-old separated mother of two teenage sons, described one situation when her son with severe asthma was younger:

He almost died. I had to come home. He had asthma at the baby-sitter's. I knew he was sick [and still sent him to child care]. ... I had to come home because the baby-sitter called me to come home, and I had to call the paramedics. But if I was the mother that I was supposed to be and being home keeping him in the house ... in his own bed, he would've been better off. I made a big mistake.

Colleen clearly blamed herself, but her situation was far from unique. We talked to many other parents who had made similar choices because they were barely getting by financially and knew their whole family would suffer if they lost crucial income or a needed job to care for one child. A number of the parents who had taken time off to care for their children's asthma exacerbations had lost essential income or their jobs, and were then blamed for not being able to support their families financially.

While parents who were not allowed leave from work to care for sick children often sent their sick children to child care and school, many child-care providers and schoolteachers had received little or no training in how to deal with children's health conditions—including asthma. As mentioned in Chapter 2, asthma is the most common chronic health problem among U.S. children, 4.8 million of whom are affected. Asthma accounts for one in six of all pediatric emergency visits in the United States. Agnes Charles described what happened when she left her daughter with a child-care provider:

> The last time she was in the hospital, I knew that she was ill and she had to go to urgent care. They gave her medication, and she still wasn't getting any better. I took her to the baby-sitter. I told her, "She has to have her medication." [The] problem is that the day-care provider doesn't give her medication when she's supposed to. Sometimes she misses it, and then [my daughter] runs into trouble. So the last time when [my daughter] was ill, I knew that if I'd been on top of everything it wouldn't have gotten that bad. She ended up having to be in the hospital for a whole week.

Her daughter was only 2 years old. At her age, Agnes's daughter couldn't describe her asthma worsening. Instead, she became increasingly upset and scared, and she cried more frequently. The baby-sitter just thought she was cranky. As soon as Agnes came to pick her up at the end of the day, she knew her daughter was having serious difficulty breathing. She could see that her daughter was retracting the front of her chest back as far as she could toward her spine just to get air in her lungs. Seeing how rapid and strained her daughter's breathing was, Agnes took her straight to the emergency room, where she was admitted to the hospital. For a week Agnes spent each night in the hospital with her daughter and each day at work. It was clear how committed she was to both her daughter and her work. But commitment wasn't enough to prevent the hospitalization in the first place when her poor working conditions and the inadequate child care available had made it impossible for Agnes to adequately care for her daughter's health while employed.

When parents consistently cared for their children's health, their jobs were often threatened. Elizabeth Carter, a 36-year-old mother of three, had a daughter, Lucy, with asthma. Elizabeth struggled to hold onto a job while meeting Lucy's needs, but Lucy was sick frequently. Elizabeth explained, "There were nights when sometimes I would go into emergency, stay with her all night, rock her in the rocking chair, and come home. My mother would watch her and [I would] go to work. How I did it, I don't know. I was half asleep, going to the store to get the medicine." Whenever possible, Elizabeth stayed at the hospital during Lucy's critical times while continuing to work; she did this by not sleeping and by having her mother's assistance. But sometimes Elizabeth had to miss work in order to be with Lucy. She described one such time: "When I had rushed her in [to the hospital] one night and it was a work night, I had stayed in. Went through emergency and I stayed in with her, just holding her and oxygen and all that. ...I just called my boss and said I wouldn't be in, and that's when everything started just going down." From that point on, her boss gave her "a lot of static." Every time Elizabeth was out, she had to bring a doctor's note to work, and her boss did everything possible to make it harder for her to continue to work. Eventually, Elizabeth said, "It was a choice— either the job or my child, and I picked my child."

Child-care providers we interviewed also had direct experience with employers who pressed parents not to care for their sick children themselves. Anne Stroble was a home day-care provider who described as typical her experience with one mother:

It was easy for the mother to get here [in terms of distance], and one day the little boy just wasn't feeling good in school. When I called her, called where she worked, they said, "Is it necessary for you talk to her?" I said, "Yes, her son is sick. I need to speak to her." After a while, she called me back and asked what's wrong. I said, "It's not an emergency, but you need to know that your son is sick. I can keep him here, but he's running a fever and he's really not himself. He's crying that he wants to go home. The more he's upset, it's not helping him." She said, "Okay." When she came to me, she said, "My boss said to me to take the rest of the day off without pay."

Thirty-four percent of parents reported that caring for their sick children led to difficulties at work; 12 percent, to lost pay; and 13 percent, to loss of promotions or jobs. For most of the families, the repercussions were serious.

Changing the Conditions Working Families Face

One parent after another told us about how *poor working conditions* and *inadequate community supports* adversely affected their children's health, education, or development. Parental *work alone* did not place children at risk. In and of itself, the entry of mothers and fathers into the wage and salary labor force did not cause the effects on children that the families in our studies described. The problem was the conditions parents faced at work and in their communities.

When families found affordable, available, quality care for their preschool and school-age children, their children fared well. The problem is that the majority of families did not find that care. When parents were able to take leave from work to care for their sick children, the children's health did not suffer. The problem was that few of the parents—part of a minority of American working parents—could consistently count on receiving paid leave and flexibility. Similarly, when parents were able to take time to meet with their children's teachers, to be at home in the evenings and supervise homework, and to help address the problems that arose, they could be resources and role models, thereby enhancing their children's development and education. But we found many parents whose work situations precluded all such possibilities.

The gap between rhetoric and reality in the United States when it comes to policies affecting families has long been large, and it is widening. While every politician claims to care deeply about families, little has been done by federal or state governments to support working parents or their children. While many companies claim they are "family friendly," few have begun to meet the needs of their employees to care for their families at unpredictable times. And many companies have fought against government efforts to fill the void in unpaid and paid leave, child and elder care. Moreover, care that used to be provided by social institutions is dramatically diminishing. Children and adults with serious diseases are spending less time in the hospital and being sent home sicker. Next to no long-term care for the mentally ill is available.

Disastrously, at the same time that little is being done to care for our nation's children or to support working families, expectations of what Americans must do in the workplace are growing. Work hours are increasing.[27] More parents have no choice but to work evening, night, and weekend shifts. Single parents living in poverty have to work long hours to support their families regardless of the age, number, health condition, or developmental needs of their children; under welfare reform, economic supports have been taken away. The cost to children and families of the widening disparities is enormous.

CHAPTER FOUR

Special Needs:
The Experience of Particularly
Vulnerable Children and Their Families

FORTY-EIGHT-YEAR-OLD Jasmine Hayes, separated from her husband, lives with two of her six children—Larissa, age 9, and Tammy, age 20. When Tammy was young and Larissa was not yet born, Jasmine worked two jobs and was able to save some money for retirement and some so she could go home for visits on vacation. Hoping to complete her GED and get a better job, she was also going to school for two hours before work. After Larissa was born, Jasmine continued to do cleaning in a hospital, but she stopped working a second shift at a nursing home and eventually had to end her schooling. She explained, "I was in the graduation class and everything. Then [Larissa] started to get sick, you know, these ear infections and nose and throat—no sleep in the nighttime. And when I get [to class], I'm sleeping and the teacher said I need to go wash my face ... so embarrassing." Often unable to arrange for any child care when Larissa was sick, Jasmine had "to call in a couple of times" to say that she needed to miss class. "I guess they got tired of me saying she is sick and there is no one [else] to take care of her. I had been telling them for a couple of weeks; they never listen. So they suspended me and said, 'You have to stay [out] for three or four weeks.' That was it." Jasmine still dreamed of going back to school but added doubtfully, "Maybe sometime next year."

Many of Larissa's illnesses were typical of those experienced by other children her age. But from birth it had been apparent that she had Down's syndrome, and the extent of her special developmental and health problems had become increasingly evident as she aged. Jasmine explained what Larissa's daily care involved:

> She's 9 years old now, and she's just like a baby. You have to give her the shower. You have to put her clothes on. You have to do everything for her, just like a baby. It's like taking care of a baby for nine years. The other kids, you stop doing stuff for them. ... They can do things on their own. You don't have to worry too much about them. With Larissa, it's never-ending.

Larissa had the body and nearly the dexterity of a 9-year-old, but she could not care for herself or recognize dangers commonly understood by a much younger child. When they were at home together, Jasmine had to watch Larissa constantly.

Outdoors, Larissa would dash out of sight. Once, for example, Jasmine had stopped to chat with a friend and had left Tammy to watch Larissa in the backyard for a few moments. When she returned, Jasmine found that Larissa had run into the middle of the street. Larissa was continually active. The disparity between her physical and cognitive development put her at risk in their apartment as well as outdoors. Because Larissa had been opening all the cabinets and then removing and breaking the contents and because she had inadvertently eaten toxic substances a few times, Jasmine had tied all the low kitchen cabinet doors shut with strings. She had also roped the kitchen chairs together so Larissa could not use them to climb up and open the high cabinets. Jasmine had had to buy a new refrigerator so that the door could be fitted with a lock, since Larissa had been constantly opening the old refrigerator and eating. Larissa had grown so obese that her doctor had begun to worry.

Jasmine often could not arrange the number of hours of quality child care she needed for Larissa. (Countless other parents face Jasmine's dilemma, since few child-care centers in the United States are well staffed or well equipped for children with disabilities.) She also had difficulty finding child-care providers or baby-sitters willing and able to care well for Larissa at home. During the day, Larissa attended a public school program for special-needs children. Jasmine cut her work hours back from forty-five to thirty-five per week because she could not find anyone to care for Larissa when she first got home from school. Jasmine's take-home pay dropped, but her responsibilities did not, since she was expected to handle her original workload. Still, she did not want to risk changing her job, because her supervisor had at least allowed her to start her afternoon and evening shift later so she could be home when Larissa arrived from school. She worked as a hospital cleaner; there was no shift that matched Larissa's school hours.

The caretakers Jasmine was able to find were frequently too inadequately trained or too inexperienced to care for Larissa well. As a result, when Jasmine was at work and someone new was baby-sitting for Larissa, Jasmine would call home five or six times a day to make sure everything was okay. If Larissa was sick and at home, Jasmine would call there ten or eleven times a day—more than once an hour—because she knew that the baby-sitters were seldom aware of how constant the oversight of Larissa needed to be. One day when Jasmine called home, Larissa was about to be taken to the emergency room because the baby-sitter had turned his back for a few moments and Larissa had eaten hair gel, causing her to break out in hives.

On weekday evenings when she had to work and Jasmine was able to find baby-sitters to care for Larissa, the baby-sitters often increased the amount of work Jasmine had to do once she got home. When Larissa was difficult to care for, the baby-sitters would put her to bed around seven in the evening, and she would sleep until eleven. When Jasmine arrived home, Larissa would awaken and stay up until two in the morning. At best, the baby-sitters kept Larissa out of danger. Jasmine still needed to bathe her, look for her clothes, and clean up. Often the baby-sitters forgot to tie the cabinets closed or lock the refrigerator, and Jasmine would come home to find salt and pepper or cooking oil on the television, hand lotion and face cream behind the television, wallets unlocatable, and fragile objects thrown downstairs and broken.

While reliable child care was more difficult to find for Larissa than it had been for Jasmine's other children, it was also more essential. Jasmine explained that the work-family balance was far more difficult with Larissa than it had been with her other children partly because Jasmine couldn't take Larissa to work in a pinch: "You can't take her to work. That's a big thing if you don't have someone to baby-sit her. When Tammy was her age and younger, I could take Tammy to work if I didn't have anybody to baby-sit her. I can't take Larissa to work with me. And I can't leave her just with anybody."

When Tammy became a mother herself, Jasmine baby-sat Tammy's newborn son as needed, and in exchange Tammy continued to care for Larissa when Jasmine needed extra help. Jasmine told us what it was like to care for Larissa and her healthy grandson together:

It's very stressful. [My grandson's] not here today. He's gone away, but when he's sitting in the chair, [Larissa will] want to go play with him. But she plays very hard, so she'll hit him, pick him up out of the crib. So I have to watch her [constantly]. It's very hard. I have to get a shower. This week she was on vacation all week [from school]. It was a tough week. They were both here and [my grandson's] mother was at work, so I had to put him in front of the door and open the door to catch a shower.

Particularly when she was caring for both her grandson and Larissa, Jasmine found it virtually impossible to handle routine tasks such as paying bills or answering correspondence.

As Jasmine detailed her life while sitting in the living room, it grew increasingly difficult to hear what she said. Larissa was coming in and out of the room, shouting, laughing, picking up Jasmine's papers, folding and crumpling them. The front door was bolted so Jasmine would not end up in the street if whoever was caring for her had a moment of inattention. Behind the door was a sign that notified anyone who might be inside to lock the door so Larissa could not get out. The couches in the living room were covered in plastic so they would not be ruined if Larissa pasted or smeared things on them. The coffee table was sticky from unidentified substances.

Although many employees return home to a "second shift"[1] during which they care for children or elderly parents, Jasmine, like other employees caring for family members with marked disabilities, was covering second and third shifts. Jasmine described her schedule as "twenty-four/seven"—working twenty-four hours a day, seven days a week. Larissa had been in diapers for nine years. When we interviewed Jasmine, she reported that lately Larissa had been taking the feces out of her diaper and smearing them all over the apartment—all over the television, the floor, the kitchen, and the living room. Jasmine would come home from work to clean up. Nothing was simple. "Disciplining her?... You see right there, see my glass," said Jasmine. "I was trying to discipline her and she breaks it. ... [She] bangs her head sometimes, if you try to tell her 'Don't do this, don't do that.'"

It was only when she was asked directly whether there were times she felt overwhelmed or tired that Jasmine responded, "Was I ever tired? I'm tired every day." Going to work was the closest thing that Jasmine had to a break. "When I go to work," she explained, "it's a big relief. The problem is behind me. It's so good to get there. When I get there, I can relax—nobody to bother me, no Larissa, no baby, nobody."

At work, during the official moments of rest, she could read a newspaper. She could also relax while she ate, which she never got to do at home. When we asked Jasmine about the impact on her own health of the caretaking burden, she responded, "I think about [my health] all the time. What will happen to [Larissa], when I die?"

Larissa Hayes's marked disability profoundly affected not only her own life but also the lives of her mother and siblings. One and a half million children and youths in the United States have severe disabilities.[2] For their parents, every aspect of balancing paid labor and family life becomes simultaneously more crucial and more risky. The work-family debates have virtually ignored both the profoundly disabled children like Larissa and the millions more whose less marked disabilities—either chronic health conditions or educational and developmental difficulties—nonetheless extensively affect the daily challenges and opportunities they and their families face.

Children with Special Health Needs

Nationwide, approximately one out of five children—a total of more than twelve million children—have special health or developmental needs.[3] Parents play critical roles in the care of children with special health needs, as shown in studies of children with epilepsy, asthma, and diabetes.[4] In diabetes management among children, parental participation and support have been found to be crucial to effective metabolic control,[5] especially as the disease is controlled through diet, blood glucose monitoring, and insulin administration.[6] The emotional support provided during the time parents are able to be with their children is as important as their instrumental support,[7] and parents play a vital role in their children's psychological adjustment to disease and medical management.[8]

The working parents we studied who had children with special health needs had to find a way to take their children to a large number of pediatric visits each year in addition to providing daily care for their children when they were sick. While the pediatric visits for all families with young children were frequent enough to create dilemmas for the parents in balancing care for their children's health and work responsibilities, the problem was particularly marked for families in which a child had special health needs. In our Urban Working Families Study, we reviewed children's medical records. In the families we studied, infants who had specific health or learning needs averaged eleven sick and well visits per year, whereas infants without specific health or learning needs averaged six sick and well visits per year. Children aged 2 to 4 who had specific health and learning needs averaged seven sick and well visits per year, compared to four visits for children the same age without such needs.

The more frequent medical care required by children with health conditions or special learning needs and the increased pressures their parents experienced were evident among many of the families mentioned in Chapters 2 and 3. Karin Arnette had to make sure that her son, Mason, took his inhaled medication; she tried to stay at home with him when he had asthma exacerbations and had to have more medication (Chapter 2). Still, she and her husband had to be prepared for the problems that signaled a need to rush Mason to the emergency room. When Mason had to be hospitalized and Karin took off from work to stay with him, her supervisor disapproved of her cutbacks. In Chapter 3, the experiences of Colleen Brown, Agnes Charles, and Elizabeth Carter—all parents of children with asthma—were described. All of these parents were torn between the needs of their children and the requirements of their jobs. In each case, lacking paid leave that they could use to care for their sick children endangered their children's health, threatened their jobs, or both.

To understand how common these problems were nationally, we used U.S. Labor Department data to examine the paid leave and work flexibility available from 1990 to 1996 to families that had children with a physical, emotional, or mental condition requiring frequent attention or treatment from a doctor, the regular use of a medicine, or the use of special physical equipment, or a condition that limited their ability to attend school regularly, do regular schoolwork, or take part in other common activities of childhood.[9] We examined the number of families in double or multiple jeopardy: Parents in double jeopardy had neither paid sick leave nor paid vacation leave with which to meet their children's health needs; those in multiple jeopardy lacked paid sick leave, paid vacation leave, and scheduling flexibility. We discovered that families with the greatest needs faced the worst working conditions. Sixty percent of working parents who had two or more children with a chronic condition at times had neither sick leave nor vacation leave, thereby experiencing double jeopardy; and 37 percent of these parents, also lacking any flexibility, were at times in multiple jeopardy. Among families who had one child with a chronic health condition, 42 percent found themselves at times in double jeopardy, and 25 percent, in multiple jeopardy. In contrast, among parents who had no children with special needs, 40 percent were in double jeopardy some of the time they worked, and 23 percent were in multiple jeopardy.

Children with Educational and Developmental Difficulties

Sofia Olivarez was born in Portugal and at age 11 immigrated with her family to the United States. Born in the middle of nine brothers and sisters, she ended up acting as a mother to many of them. When we interviewed her, at age 32, she had a 10-year-old son, Joseph, and a 7-year-old son, Jesse. Sofia's mother lived only a couple of blocks away, but it was Sofia who cared for her mother, not her mother who helped Sofia care for her children. Sofia went grocery shopping for her mother, paid her bills, scheduled her doctors' appointments, and took her to them.

For ten years Sofia had worked as an assembler in an electronics plant before being laid off. After being unemployed for six months, she went back to school to get training as a medical assistant. She liked helping people with their health care and hoped the training would better position her to compete in the job market. She was married, but her husband, a tow truck driver, contributed neither the time nor the money required to raise the children. His life was largely separate from the family's. Raising her children virtually on her own, Sofia faced constant work:

> When you're watching a movie, you'd think, "Oh my God, don't I wish to be there?" I don't know. My life is very hard, I would say. …It's just that I work. I come home. It's almost the same routine. You cook, you clean, take care of the kids, do homework. You go to bed, who knows when. You get up early in the morning. The same routine, over and over again. Weekends … it's just the housework, to get ready for the next day to go to work.

When asked how much time she got to spend on an average day to take care of her personal needs, Sofia simply responded, "None."

Of course, on days when one of her children was sick or any of the predictable interruptions of children's lives arose, the demands were even higher. Then she often didn't sleep: "There's lots of times that I remember that I was up almost the whole night, rocking them to sleep. And then you still have to get up to go to work the next day. Those times were hard." In addition to caring for her children, Sofia helped her mother-in-law care for one of Sofia's nieces, who frequently got ear infections.

But the greatest challenges Sofia faced were due to her son's learning difficulties. Every year, at the beginning of the school year, Jesse wouldn't want to go to school. He would cry for days on end. He just wanted to stay home. For two and a half years before any diagnosis was made, it was clear to Jesse and Sofia that something was wrong. Finally, in the midst of second grade, Jesse was diagnosed with learning disabilities. The frustrations Jesse faced as he tried to learn had seemed inexplicable before. While it had become clear why he was so frustrated, it still was far from clear how to help him:

> When I get home, I hear complaints that [Jesse] doesn't want to do [his homework]. Whenever I come home, I sit him down and talk to him and tell him, "What is wrong? This is what you have to do." But he says, he doesn't know how. ... Like today, before you came, [I said,] "You have to do this. You have to put this in alphabetical order. ...Write the whole alphabet here, and you can take the list and look and see which word comes first." He started the alphabet, and he came to the letter E. He started crying, and I said, "Jesse, you're in second grade, and you don't know the alphabet."

Jesse would have been a difficult child to teach regardless of his parents' working conditions. Sofia would have needed help knowing how to teach Jesse to read and do schoolwork. But Sofia had to work two evenings a week. Working conditions that were difficult but might have been manageable if none of her children were having difficulty in school had serious consequences for Sofia's ability to help Jesse. Jesse was left with his older brother. Having no adult to help Jesse with homework those evenings made things worse. Sofia had no choice about her schedule, not if she was going to keep her job. "Every day when I go to work, they ask me, 'Mom, are you coming home late?' And [if I will be] the oldest ... does his homework. But I tell Jesse, 'Jesse, I'm going to get home at a certain time. Try to do your homework, and [Joseph] will help you. If you have any problems, you save it for me.'" Jesse, however, did no schoolwork when left with his brother, and he finished some only if one of his parents was at home to assist. The school was talking about requiring Jesse to repeat second grade.

Sofia's and Jesse's experiences of parental work conditions conflicting with children's needs are common among families in which a child faces developmental, behavioral, or school difficulties. While the provisions available to working parents for addressing the health needs of their children are currently inadequate, virtually no attention has been paid to ensuring that ways exist for parents of children with special educational needs to work at the same time as meeting the needs of their children.

Learning disabilities are the single most prevalent form of disability among U.S. children.[10] At least one in thirteen children is estimated to have a learning disability, and in any given year, one in nineteen children in the public schools receives services for an identified learning disability.[11] Thus, even using conservative estimates, over two million children in the United States and their families are affected substantially. Learning disabilities significantly affect not only the children themselves but also their parents, their siblings, and other family members.[12] The impact of learning disabilities has been observed not only in the United States but internationally.[13]

Children with learning disabilities have the same range of abilities, intelligence, and talents as children without such conditions. What distinguishes them is that the way their minds work makes learning academic subjects—in the way they are currently taught in schools— more difficult. When educational programs are not well adapted to meet the needs of children with learning disabilities or differences, the consequences can be devastating for their school, work, and life outcomes. Most children with special educational needs share several characteristics: They are harder to raise, they take more attention to teach, and—given adequate support—they can do as well as any children. The cost to them and to society of ignoring their needs is enormous—far greater than the price of addressing their needs well. Even with inadequate services, some children and youth with learning disabilities have fared extremely well. But when services are poor and parents' working conditions are worse, many children who could succeed don't. At present, as a nation, we are failing many of our children with learning disabilities.

Even before high school, children with learning disabilities are far more likely to fail a class; one study showed nearly half of learning-disabled seventh graders had failed a course.[14] Nearly 40 percent of learning-disabled children do not complete high school,[15] and for every three learning-disabled students aged 16 to 21 who graduate from secondary school or receive a certificate of completion, one drops out of school.[16] Three to five years after completing high school, only 27 percent of learning-disabled youths are enrolled in postsecondary school, compared to 68 percent of nondisabled youths, 57 percent of all visually impaired youths, and 60 percent of all hard-of-hearing or deaf youths.[17] Even among those who finish high school, only 37 percent of learning-disabled youths had enrolled in postsecondary school, compared with 78 percent of those without learning disabilities. Furthermore, those youths with learning disabilities who go on to postsecondary education are likely to be more pessimistic about how they will fare academically, even when they have grade point averages equivalent to those of students without learning disabilities.[18] Those who do not graduate from high school are less likely to find full-time jobs, more likely to be either underemployed or unemployed, and more likely to get lower wages.[19] Across a range of settings, young women with learning disabilities are even less likely to be employed after high school than men with similar difficulties.[20]

Children with learning disabilities often face social as well as academic challenges. When children with learning disabilities are placed in programs where their talents and efforts are valued, they thrive.[21] However, when learning disabilities are stigmatized, both children's academic achievement and their social development suffer, as does their self-confidence.[22] As a result of stigmatization, children with learning disabilities are less likely to have peers they can turn to for help with a problem.[23]

Early intervention and parental support make a difference.[24] When children receive services early, they are more likely to succeed in school. But in the United States, children are often diagnosed late. And among children who are not identified until they are 9 or older, three-quarters continue to read in the bottom fifth of their class throughout high school.[25] A study in Michigan found that nearly three out of four students with learning disabilities had been made to repeat a grade before they were even referred for a learning disability evaluation,[26] thus decreasing their chances of ever graduating from high school.[27] Furthermore, parents often lack any possibility of providing their children with the level of assistance they need.

In our study of children with special educational needs in which we interviewed employed parents of children with school problems, more than half of the parents reported that working conditions made it difficult or impossible for them to help their children with schoolwork in the ways needed. George Parker, like many other parents, could not even take time off on one day to visit his son's school and then compensate by working more hours the next day. His son, Matt, was smart. George could tell, and Matt's teacher could tell. Matt could remember every story covered in school and recite the plot months later. He learned math with ease and was multiplying and dividing when his classmates were still struggling with subtracting. But Matt still could not write. He learned to write his name almost two years after most of his friends. By now his friends were sitting down and writing stories, simple short stories, but stories nonetheless. He was still struggling to write down words in a form recognizable enough that ten minutes later he would know what he had written. George knew Matt needed extra help, and he knew that with help Matt would catch up. Matt's teachers assured him of that. As a first step, the teachers wanted Matt to get evaluated for learning disabilities. George, however, could not get needed time off from work to take Matt to an evaluation or to help arrange for a tutor. Even if George's job had allowed for unpaid time off, George could not have afforded to take it, particularly since he needed to find money for extra tutoring for Matt.

Lack of control over their work schedules, like lack of paid leave and inflexibility, often left parents unable to provide essential help. As was the case for Jesse when Sofia Olivarez had to work evenings, mandatory evening work forced other parents, like Alexandra Taylor, to make an untenable choice between their need for a job and their children's need for help with schoolwork. Alexandra Taylor, a single mother of two, explained that her learning-disabled son, Daniel, had great difficulty doing his homework: "I knew that with repetition he was bound to get it if he wanted to," she said. "After he stopped fighting me, he would pick it up. He wouldn't pick it up quickly, but it was about repetition." While he was able to get schoolwork done when his mother was home, no after-school program designed for children with special needs was available, and her son could not get his work done alone:

> If I had to work the evenings, I would call and I would ask my mother or my father, "Can you go ...?" When we first found out about the disability, I would say, "Can you go over [the schoolwork] with him? He knows he has to repeat it." So I would explain to him, I'd explain to my parents, and they would just go by what I said, you know. And then I called them one day and my father ... goes, "You know, he's crying, right? He's crying, and he said he doesn't want to do it." I said, "Tell him sorry, but he has to do it." ... [My father] was upset.

While she was fortunate to have her own parents available to attempt to fill the void left by the absence of adequate after-school programs, her parents had neither the training, the experience, nor the tenacity to get her learning-disabled son through his schoolwork.

One out of four parents we interviewed felt impeded when trying to make appointments with specialists. As the distance between the parents' workplaces and their children's schools or specialists' offices increased, the work-related scheduling difficulties for the parents mounted, since they had to plan on more time for the necessary travel. Low-income parents who had no car and relied on multiple bus connections or parents who worked far from their children's schools faced especially serious problems. Anna Solarino, a 34-year-old low-income single mother of three, had a son with learning disabilities and a daughter with asthma. She was working as an administrative assistant and said it was virtually impossible to make the school meetings she was supposed to attend for her son at eleven o'clock in the morning: "Occasionally the principal would want to talk to me about something. …How can I do that?… What am I going to do? Go all the way home and come all the way back [afterwards, to work] just to meet with [the principal]? You know I couldn't do that."

The combined problems caused by parents' work conditions and inadequate transportation meant that some young children were traveling by themselves. Natalie Dumas, a 35-year-old married mother of two who was working full-time as a home health aide, described her 7-year-old son Clarence's visits to be evaluated for his learning disability. She got out of work at four, and the latest appointment she could get for her son was at five o'clock. "My mother put Clarence on the bus," she explained. "Then I met him at Harvard Square. [My mother gave] a little note to the bus driver, and I would wait at the station for him." Even with these efforts, they barely made the last available appointment. "I have to kill myself to try to be there on time. It's very hard," Natalie concluded.

The routine care of children with special developmental needs is often not routine. LaDonna Andrews, a single mother working both a full-time and a part-time job to make ends meet, described what it was like to get her son with attention deficit disorder (ADD) ready for school each morning:

I constantly have to remind him, constantly have to be after him, even with small tasks like getting dressed, brushing your teeth, combing your hair. ...I'll be in the kitchen, start making lunches, and twenty minutes later he's still in bed. He hasn't brushed his teeth. Now I have to leave what I'm doing, go get him out of bed, get him in the bathroom, get him brushing his teeth, get back to what I'm doing. ...He's in the bathroom for a half an hour playing in the faucet. ...I take him to the room, put some clothes on him ... get his socks, underwear, T-shirt, lay it all out on the bed. Now it's like, he can go and he can pick his own shirt and his own stuff to put on. It's getting him into the clothes that's the task.

Moreover, parents of children with developmental difficulties faced additional challenges helping their children on special as well as routine occasions. One 12-year-old boy with learning disabilities had trouble focusing in class, and on school field trips he did not always stay with the group. His mother, Susan Hamilton, explained, "One day he almost got caught on the train, in between the doors, and it was, 'Mrs. Hamilton, if you don't come, then he can't go.'" From that point on, the school gave Susan no choice: Instead of providing her son with needed supports, they stipulated that if her son was to go on field trips, she would have to attend every one. The school never considered what that meant for Susan—a divorced mother of three who had to work fifty hours a week to support her family—or for her children.

Crises occur more frequently, as well as at any hour of the day or night, among children with special needs. Josephina Fiore, a separated mother of three who worked as a housecleaner, described how early in her son's life the challenges of raising a child with ADD were evident:

My son was three-and-a-half. He jumped out the window there [she said, pointing to a window in her apartment]. Two-thirty in the morning, you know, I'm hearing a baby crying. I said, "Where's that kid coming from?"

I've been looking around. At the time, I had a big bureau or something like that up against the window, one of those big mirrors. He actually pushed it out of the way. He jumped out the window—not a scratch. ... It was five degrees below out. The door downstairs was locked. What if I didn't hear him? What would've happened to him? I was working then, so I was up all night that night. Because he was sleeping maybe an hour in the night, I would have to be around the clock awake. I found him one morning, four o'clock in the morning, fell asleep out in the backyard playing in the snow. I had to take my washing machine, start putting it up against the door so he couldn't get out.

In sum, parents caring for children with learning difficulties, developmental problems, or behavioral problems work far more than a second shift. Working, parenting, and meeting special needs were at times clearly too much for the parents we interviewed to deal with. Fatigue and stress affected the way parents dealt with their children and the extent to which they were able to help with the extra tasks their children's needs involved. They needed a day off from work to help their children throughout the day instead of having to handle three jobs back-to-back: doing their paid work, parenting, and meeting their children's special needs. Fatigue limited parents' involvement with schools. For some, like Anna Solarino, the problem wasn't just scheduling meetings but fatigue. "By the time I get home, I'm dead."

While the experiences of parents of children with academic problems have much in common with the experiences of those whose children have emotional or behavioral problems, there are also important differences in the problems they face. The differences have important implications for how children fare in school as well as for how parents fare in the workplace. Academic problems necessitate that children get help with homework and have the chance to see specialists. To get this help, children need an adult available who has the time, resources, and ability to ensure the child's educational requirements are being met. When communities fail to provide supports outside of school hours, working parents need to have either time off during the school week to address these issues or ways of finding and affording someone to help. When the parents we studied were unavailable, children often did not receive the services they needed. They fell behind academically. They did not achieve their potential. Perhaps most dangerously, often no school personnel called parents as their children began sliding further behind.

In contrast, schools called parents frequently when their children had behavioral problems. Consequently, parents had frequent interruptions at work, cutbacks, and difficulty finding and keeping jobs. But because these interruptions often came without a helpful plan for how to address the children's needs, they often negatively affected the parents' work without necessarily helping the children. LaDonna Andrews, for example, was receiving regular calls from her son's school about his ADD. LaDonna described her own experience even when she did not have to leave work:

> I just feel this constant, constant stress. Most of the time I'm able to kind
> of push it aside, leave it at the door. Then other days it just travels with
> me to work. Occasionally I'm very distracted—like the memory loss
> thing. It's not memory loss, but I'm so distracted I don't remember to do
> things or what I did with them or how I got there.

Even supervisors who understood parents' need to meet other family responsibilities did not always understand their need to address the issues involving children with developmental problems. Wendy Johnson, an employed 40-year-old mother of four, described a recent difficulty when her son Joey was at camp and "flew off the handle because he spilt milk on himself." She said, "They called me and asked me can I come and get him. I told [my boss] at two o'clock, 'Marsha, I have to leave.'" Wendy explained that her son was frustrated enough with himself that small things would set off his problems. "Joey can bring it on himself. He can be sitting down eating and he drops something. He gets so mad with himself. Joey can try to have a conversation and the words just aren't coming out the way that he wants them to and he'll go off. So it can happen any time." Each workday, Wendy hoped no interruptions, such as phone calls, would occur. But they did happen often, and that left her in the position of being viewed as irresponsible by either her job supervisor or Joey's school.

In our studies, the ability of schools to support working families, even in simple matters, varied greatly between communities and even among schools within a given community. The school LaDonna Andrews's son attended could not even ensure that he made it onto the bus. LaDonna recounted:

> There were a couple of incidents where he didn't get on the school bus, and they found him at 3:30 or 4:00 out on the courtyard by himself. ... At the age of a kindergartner or first grader, there should be an adult waiting with them to be sure that they get on that bus. They were like, "We're not responsible for putting the kids on the bus." You must be crazy! Who is responsible for my child until he gets on the bus and then another adult is responsible for him? Who's responsible for him?

Nor were services effectively coordinated to meet his needs during the school day. LaDonna explained, "The Ritalin, he had to take it three or four times a day. ...And people would mess up." Sometimes, for instance, a teacher would give an extra, unneeded dose because LaDonna's son, who was behaving disruptively, said he had not had his medication and the teacher did not call to check with LaDonna. "There was one time," said LaDonna, "when ... everybody was giving him medication and no one checked with the other person. And I thought they were going to overdose my son." Despite the lack of calls to discuss medication needs, LaDonna said that the school was calling her almost every day to come pick up her son. Consequently, her son often did not get to go to school, and she often had to miss work, even though the family relied on her as the only source of income. The lack of effective support and services dramatically affected the whole family.

After-school teachers and child-care providers also reported the difficulty they had providing adequate care for children with special needs at existing staffing levels. Children with special needs received extra support during the school day because of state and federal laws and regulations,[28] but they often received little or no extra support when they attended preschool or after-school care. Heather Tillery, a teacher in a public urban after-school program, explained:

> They're just children like anybody else. They are wonderful and also aggravating, like any other kid can be. ... But these kids definitely take a lot of one-on-one attention and a lot of energy devoted just for them. Sometimes I feel like we need another aide. We need a special aide just for those kids. The kid that we have now that has ADD, his [school-day] classroom has fourteen kids and four teachers. They have a ratio of one to three. You know, it's amazing. Then they come here [to after-school care] and we have twenty-six kids and three teachers. ...The support for these kids stops at two-thirty [in the afternoon].

When children with special academic needs are in understaffed preschools and after-school care, one of three things occurs: First, the children's special needs go unaddressed, and these children fall farther behind their peers who can, with less supervision, learn preschool skills or complete assigned work after school. Second, extra attention is provided to the children with special academic needs, but at the cost of other children in the program, who then receive less supervision than they require. Third, the special-needs children are excluded from a program or asked to attend for a shorter day—as is often the case when the emotional or behavioral aspects of the special needs mean that teachers cannot ignore the problems. Moreover, the problems caused by understaffing are exacerbated by the limited training most teachers and child-care providers have in how to help children with special needs.

Implications

In the United States, none of the social programs or institutions designed to serve children with special needs have adjusted to the fact that the majority of these children's parents work in the paid labor force. While employers have been ignoring the needs of the millions of families in which a child has a chronic condition or disability, educators and health-care providers serving these children have been ignoring the need of their parents to work. The manner in which learning disability specialists are typically scheduled to work with students provides one example of schools' unresponsiveness: As the experiences of the families we interviewed made clear, children with learning disabilities commonly need help after school. Right now, in many school districts, children with special needs are pulled out of regular classes between 9:00 A.M. and 2:00 P.M. to meet with specialists, while no services are offered after school. During these "pull-out" sessions, the children often miss important material in regular classes and thus fall farther behind. If some of the specialists' hours were shifted to after-school sessions, then children would be able both to get help after school and to miss fewer regular classes. This straightforward change would help both working families and their children with special needs—at little or no additional cost to school systems. But even this change has not been implemented because schools have not yet begun to respond to the twentieth century's major demographic shifts in labor-force participation.

In fact, ignoring the reality of families, many health and educational programs are currently placing increasing burdens on families during workdays. For example, recent trends in health-care delivery have significantly increased the reliance of children with special health needs on parental care. Services once provided well on an inpatient basis are now being provided on an outpatient basis to save insurance companies money, hospital stays have been significantly shortened, and children who used to spend time in rehabilitative or other health-care institutions are being sent home. In each of these cases, the burden of care is being shifted from health-care professionals and institutions to families—who are receiving far too little societal support.

While parents of children with special health and developmental needs are expected to extend extraordinary efforts to care for their children—to provide more extensive support than both parents of children without special needs and parents from recent generations who had children with special needs—the realities of the workplace often make it impossible for these parents to meet basic needs, much less additional ones. The evidence from our studies is clear: A significant number of parents who have children with special needs have neither the paid leave nor the worktime flexibility they must have to care for their children adequately. Lack of paid leave and flexibility is affecting the ability of parents to support their families, continue at work, and care for their own health. And parents whose children have the most serious—and often multiple—problems, such as Jasmine Hayes and her daughter Larissa, are currently in the greatest jeopardy. Not only are their children's needs the most extensive and unrelenting, but their working conditions are the worst. Providing adequate social supports and ensuring suitable working conditions are important for all families, but especially so for those living in poverty. Low-income children are much more likely to have significant problems with their health and development than their peers who are not living in poverty.[29] And as noted earlier, these children are more likely to have parents who lack paid leave, cannot afford unpaid leave, and cannot afford to pay for the essential children's services our nation has failed to provide. Unless policies are developed to address all of these problems, they are likely to grow as the number of children being raised in households in which all adults present work outside the home rises and the number of children living with chronic conditions increases.

CHAPTER FIVE

Impact Across the Life Span: Extended Family Fantasies and Realities

MONA VALENTIN, an office worker, began raising her son, Peter, on her own, after his father walked out when Peter was one and a half. Regretting the separation from Peter, his father came back long enough for Mona to become pregnant again. Seeing her pregnant and not wanting to take responsibility for the children, he left for good. Her daughter, Anna, was three years younger than Peter. Mona told us, with working and caring for her children, "The only time I have for myself is when I go to church." As a single parent, Mona was fatigued to the point of exhaustion. Sometimes she would force herself to read to her son and daughter, but often doing that was one task more than she could handle. The working conditions she faced—especially her boss's attitudes—didn't make it easy to be with her children when they needed her. She explained, "All [my supervisor] used to say all the time was, 'I hate kids. I hate kids.' ... And if you tell her about your kid ... it's like she doesn't care if the kid's sick or anything."

When Peter and Anna were younger, Mona asked her mother to come live with them for a while and care for the children. Mona hoped, with that help, to be able to complete nursing school and then help others address their health needs. She also wanted to earn a living wage that would enable her to work fewer hours and to spend more time with her children while financially supporting them.

After her mother came, Mona went to nursing school. She worked during the days, studied at night, and cared for her children in between. Then her mother became sick and—as happens in many families—went from being able to help to needing help. In fact, the caretaking she required was extensive. Since Mona's mother wouldn't eat any of the food the home health aides prepared, Mona would wake up at five in the morning to cook food for her mother to eat that day, even on days when she hadn't gotten to bed the night before until two or three in the morning. Mona had to quit school because she had no time; there was no choice. She used her lunch break to pick Peter up from school and take him to an after-school program. "Every day, I don't have lunch. I eat at my desk. Or if I don't bring anything to work, I stop on the streets, getting something very quick to eat," she explained. Nor did she have any vacation time: "Sometimes I get so mad. This [employee is] out for two weeks. That one's out for three weeks. This one's out for a week. I'm always there. You know, because I can't accrue any time ... I never get a vacation, never plan a vacation. My only vacation was when they were out sick or I was sick. That was the only vacation I had." All of the limited paid leave she accrued—sick or vacation—went to caring for her family. She simply did not receive enough leave to cover their needs.

With benefits at work but not enough, with access to some child care but not enough, with access to some community supports but not enough, Mona was trying to do what made the most sense while raising two children on her own and working. "That's why I had thought about sending for my mother. ...We were so happy when she came so that she could help me with them," she recalled. "Then she couldn't help herself for so long." Mona's ill mother never slept, so Mona was up most nights with her. Mona's mother lived with her for a year, before returning to Haiti to die.

But the last straw came when Anna, then a preschooler, was hospitalized for two weeks after Mona's mother had become sick. Scared of the hospital crib, scared of the hospital chairs, scared of everyone who walked in the room, Anna would sleep only if she lay down on top of Mona. Exhausted from caring for her mother day and night, Mona would lie on her back and put her daughter on her chest or rock her in a chair. Afterwards, Mona collapsed from some combination of exhaustion and depression. Mona left work on short-term disability and was home for a month recovering. Her sister lived hundreds of miles away—too far away to help on a routine basis—but was loving enough to drop everything and come in an emergency, so she cared for Anna and Peter while Mona saw doctors and recovered. After a month, Mona returned to work and to caring for Anna and Peter alone.

Extended Family as Caregivers

One of the fantasies in the United States is that grandmothers and extended families fill all the voids left by the absence of quality, affordable child care. The grandmother of these fairy tales is not in the labor force. She does not need to work for pay, since her husband— who is healthy and does not need her care—is employed and well paid. She lives near all her grandchildren and is instantly available to care for them at any time. She no longer has any of her own children at home. Her own parents, her in-laws, and her other relatives aren't even part of the fantasy, since they are not sick, disabled, extremely elderly, or for any other reason in need of care. The fantasy grandmother's own health is remarkably good: She is well enough, strong enough, and fit enough to act like a parent while raising her grandchildren. Moreover, unlike what we assume of a grandfather at this point in his life, she does not have work, a career, or community involvements that she wants to continue. Oh yes, and unlike what we assume about paid work, she will never retire from unpaid caretaking.

While extended family members are a great source of many not-so-minor miracles, they rarely look like the cast of this extended fantasy. Grandparents are available to help on a daily basis in only a small minority of families. Some of those are like Mary Webster, 66, and her husband, Jerome, 75, who had three children and eleven grandchildren. They lived around the corner from their oldest daughter's family and down the street from their youngest daughter's house. Mary had retired, and each day she cared for one of her daughter's children when they came home from school. (There were too many grandchildren and their needs were too disparate for her to be able to help with her other daughter's children at the same time.)

But while some grandparents are able to take care of some of their grandchildren, others are too tired, too busy caring for multiple people at the same time, working full-time, or having intractable battles with their children over how to raise the grandchildren. Health problems frequently limit the extent, nature, and duration of caregiving by grandparents. Widowed, Lucia Sandalo cared for five of her grandchildren, aged 8 to 14 years old. Her own six children were all adults. While she was willing to care for her grandchildren, she explained, "I have days when I'm perfectly fine. Then I have other days when I can hardly walk."

Eve Smith's adult daughter was paralyzed in an automobile accident, and from that point on, Eve cared for her daughter and for her grandson. Eve has multiple sclerosis, and as is true for many others who have the disease, her neurologic difficulties were exacerbated by overwork and fatigue. Still, she had managed to care for her own serious health problems while working in customer service at a publishing company. But caring for her grieving, newly wheelchair-bound daughter and her grandson was putting her over the edge. Eve described to us how caring for her daughter and grandson was damaging her own health:

> This is our busy season—so I've been basically working about twenty hours overtime a week as well as my regular workweek. I'm trying to deal with my daughter, my grandchild … and now my health is going down. … I got sick Thursday. Really sick. By four-thirty in the afternoon—I had to do a lot of writing—I could not even hold a pen to write because [the multiple sclerosis] was affecting my hands. The stress works through my nervous system. Friday I had to take the day off. I had to go into the doctor's, had all these tests run. Now I'll go in Monday, and they'll pump me through with steroids all week long.

Government subsidies that would have been available to Eve to help with her grandson's child care, because of her low-income, had she been the mother were unavailable to her as the grandmother.

Frequently, grandparents who once were well enough to help care for their children's children develop health problems as they age that prevent them from providing further assistance. Karin Arnette (see Chapter 2) explained simply what many parents experienced: "My mother, when her health wasn't as bad as it is now, she would come over sometimes and baby-sit." But the baby-sitting stopped when her mother's health went downhill. Even grandparents in good health, though, fatigue more readily as they age, and this change limits the nature and amount of time they spend caring for grandchildren. An office assistant and divorced mother of three, Tracey Edelman described this phenomenon with her mother, whose caretaking help Tracey greatly appreciated: "She's been wonderful. She'll pick [the children] up if she can. But lately she's been tired. … I don't ask too much of her." Instead, her children increasingly stayed home with each other, and Tracey would call from work to check on them periodically. Tracey's experience was common. Cynthia Kingston, a 34-year-old separated mother of two young children with asthma, similarly explained, "I hate to rely on my mother so much, because I do. I'm trying to stop doing that. So the less I ask her to do—come down and sit with the kids—it's better, because she's tired. Everyone's so worn out." As grandparents age, parents are also hesitant to ask their help caring for sick children, lest the grandparents become dangerously ill. A cafeteria worker and mother of two, Susanna Charles said her parents pitched in with child-care duties. However, she explained, "When [my son] got scarlet fever, I didn't want [his grandmother] to mind him, because I was scared she'd get something."

Many adults live too far from their parents and siblings, who might otherwise help with child care. At 53 years old, Gene Denison explained that he thought his 2-year-old son would have a better relationship with his grandparents if they lived nearby, but his grandparents lived in other states. The same was true for Elaine Laredo, a 16-year-old mother of one whose father was dead and whose mother lived halfway across the country—more than a day's drive away. The possibilities for directly assisting with caregiving diminish whenever parents, grandparents, aunts, uncles, and siblings have to move to another part of the country in order to take a job, find affordable housing, seek better opportunities, or simply make ends meet. But Elaine and Gene at least had family in the United States. While some immigrants have a great deal of extended family in the United States, other immigrants face particular barriers to working while raising their children because the majority of their family resides in their country of origin. A 33-year-old mother of a 4-year-old with chronic ear problems and an infant son, Debbie Lee knew from her siblings and from their temporary visit that having grandparents around could be a tremendous help, but her parents' home was in China.

Family support structures after divorce are as varied as family supports before divorce. A great deal of attention has been paid to the range of involvement of noncustodial parents—still predominantly fathers—after a divorce. Some are involved in their children's lives daily or weekly; others, rarely or never. But the consequences of divorce reverberate past parents to grandparents and to other extended-family members. While some remain involved, others do not. At 33 years old, Carola Suarez worked as a nurse's assistant in the public schools while caring for her two children, Pedro and Belinda, both of whom had asthma. Carola Suarez explained that her mother-in-law would no longer help her with the grandchildren after her divorce. Carola had only twenty to thirty dollars a week available for child care.

Divorce was not the only factor that strained relationships. Emily Larson had little involvement with her own biological family: "I have contact with them, but it's not always what I want to hear when I call. When my mother calls me, it's always fighting."

How grandparents support themselves is obviously a critical determinant of the extent to which they can help care for grandchildren, but for some reason, the relationship between paid work and grandparenting work is rarely discussed. Glenn Baxter explained simply, "My parents play a minor role. ...Both are working full-time right now too, so it's kind of hard." While the increasingly wide age range at which Americans first become parents—commonly, between the teens and the forties—creates great diversity in the ages of grandparents, half of grandparents are younger than 60, and the majority of these are in the labor force.[1] The average age at which Americans become grandparents for the first time is 47, and among people that age, 75 percent of women and 89 percent of men are in the labor force.[2] Although past trends had involved declining paid employment among older adults due to the availability of Social Security and pensions, current trends are for higher levels of labor-force participation as rules against age discrimination lead to the elimination of mandatory retirement and as the security of retirement incomes declines.

By and large, it is only those grandparents and other extended-family members who are not working for pay outside the home who can routinely help with child care. Roslyn Eaton was a married 38-year-old teacher and the mother of Elgin, age 3, and Mario, age 1. When Elgin was born, Roslyn's brother Joseph was unemployed and was living with Roslyn and her husband, so Joseph cared for Elgin while Roslyn and her husband worked. Joseph continued providing care for five months, until he found a job. Then Roslyn and her husband needed to find child care from outside their family.

Adults and Elders Who Need Care

Older family members are as often in need of assistance themselves as they are able to provide it, and older Americans have for some time been the fastest growing population group. Between 1870 and 1990, the U.S. population increased sixfold, but the population of Americans 65 years old and older increased twenty-seven-fold.[3] The impact is great both on the absolute number of older people and on the proportion of the total population they represent. In 1870, those 65 years and older accounted for just over one million Americans (3 percent of the population).[4] As of 1999, there were more than thirty-four million older Americans (13 percent of the population).[5] By the year 2030, the U.S. Bureau of the Census estimates that there will be approximately seventy million people 65 and older (20 percent of the population).[6] The increasing needs of an aging population are not unique to the United States. By 1990, people 65 years or older accounted for 16 percent of the respective populations in Norway and the United Kingdom and for more than 12 percent of the respective populations in Japan, the Netherlands, and Hungary.[7]

Older individuals live enormously varied lives. Some are in superb health. Some continue working for pay or caring for children or grandchildren more than full-time and leading a fully active life both physically and mentally. Because of chronic conditions or disabilities, others face significant limitations in the work they can do, the care they can provide others, or the extent to which they can manage their daily lives themselves. Although a great range of experience exists among older individuals, they are more likely than younger people to have limitations in their activities and in their ability to care for themselves. While fewer than one in thirty-five working-age adults have limitations in their ability to care for themselves, one in six adults 65 years old or older who are not living in institutions have difficulty bathing, dressing, getting around inside or outside their home, or with other activities essential to living independently.[8] Only a small minority of 60- and 70-year-olds have significant limitations, but the probability of having health problems increases with age.

Few of those who have been termed the "young-old"—people aged 65 to 74, who often are fit enough to help significantly with caregiving—live with their adult children and grandchildren.[9] In fact, only 4 percent of older men and 8 percent of older women live with a family member other than their spouse.[10] Only 2 percent of older men and 6 percent of older women live with their children or children-in-law. The number of the "old-old"—those 75 years old and older, who are far more likely to need help themselves—living with their adult children or other family member is significantly higher; among people over 85, the frequency doubles.[11]

Many working adults need to care for both their parents and their children. A Spanish teacher in a private school, Karla Maldonado was raising Eldon, a son with asthma. She described what it was like when her mother-in-law lived with her family: "I felt like I was working more, taking care of her, going to work and trying to keep up with everything and [give] attention to my son. It was very stressful. Even though at the same time I felt good doing it, it was very stressful. It was very stressful," she emphasized. Similarly, a 44-year-old social worker,

Caroline Hardin, explained what caring for her father-in-law for the three years before he died was like: "We had to do all his shopping, and we'd take him for walks because he was blind. He couldn't do that by himself. Then he eventually had a stroke, and then he really needed full-time care. He became incontinent, and we ... got a hospice to come in and help twice a day. But we were doing really heavy duty care." At the time, her children were 8 and 9 years old. Another parent, Regina Percell, a 26-year-old single mother of 4-year-old and one-and-a-half-year-old sons, was working twenty hours a week and attending school full-time to try to make it out of poverty. Regina's mother was helping care for the children but had deteriorating health and needed Regina's help in making multiple visits to the doctor.

Caring for elderly parents markedly affects adults' work. Colleen Brown cared for her mother, who had Alzheimer's disease, for nine years. Separated from her children's father, she was raising two sons on her own while working full-time doing data entry. During the first five of the nine years that she helped care for her mother, her mother and father still lived together. But her father relied on Colleen for help—even when someone needed to bring her mother in from the street at three o'clock in the morning because she had become confused and lost. When the strain of living with and caring for a spouse with Alzheimer's led her father to have a nervous breakdown, Colleen also cared for him. When each parent was in a nursing home—her mother, for the last four years of her life; her father, for rehabilitation—Colleen provided companionship, did their laundry, and came in for all major medical decisions. For Colleen, the times her mother urgently needed assistance meant work absences during the day and fatigue at work the next day when the need occurred in the middle of the night. Similar strains confronted Nina Martinez, a married, middle-class, 43-year-old teacher whose mother developed ovarian cancer when Nina's daughter was 1-year old. Nina had to face a tremendous caretaking load while grieving: "I would take [my mother] to chemotherapy three times a week. ...There was a time she looked fine. Then it came back. She died in nine months. The problem with her disease was the last month before she died. ...She was very ill. She couldn't walk."

The experience of having one parent grow sick after the other is common. When the husband or wife in a close relationship dies, the strain can significantly affect the remaining spouse's health. The morning Nina's mother died, her father had a heart attack. "So I left my mother in one room," Nina explained. "She just passed away, and [I] went down to the emergency room with him. ...They thought that he was going to die. So, I just died [inside. He was] that sick. There is a social worker there [at the hospital], and she came with me. She never left me alone, and she said, 'This is more than anyone can really take.'" It was more than Nina could take. She explained, "I remember once I went to my classroom and I thought that everything was closing in on me and I left. I left the kids by themselves."

While caring for elderly parents is the most common kind of adult caregiving responsibility, the range of adults cared for is wide. A secretary, Edie Vogel lived with her husband, their three children, and an 80-year-old family friend. The 80-year-old had been a friend of her family for as long as she could remember; in fact, he'd been such a close friend that her parents had named her after him. When he developed emphysema and other health problems, it was only natural that she take care of him, since he had no one else who could do so. She took Ed to doctor's appointments and increasingly helped him meet his basic daily needs; at the same time, she was caring for one daughter's health problems—repeated ear infections and respiratory problems—and another's learning disability.

Kathleen Denison cared for her 2-year-old son, Craig, as well as her husband, Gene, who had multiple sclerosis, which left him progressively disabled. Caring for him affected her work and her ability to care for their son. A caterer, she was once serving a large group when she found out that her husband had fallen and needed her to come home to help him. She went home immediately and returned to work after she had cared for him. Sometimes she would have two back-to-back appointments in a day, but she would still run home in between them to help her husband go to the bathroom or get dressed. She gave an example of how such efforts also affected her ability to care for her son:

> I absentmindedly put [Craig] in the car while I rushed to get Gene, and I didn't strap [my son] into his car seat, which I should've done. I rushed to get Gene because I was worried about him. ... [My son] crawled into the front seat and picked up a bottle of No-Doze [which are potentially toxic]. ... I think the larger issue at the time was this—the way my loyalties were divided. Who do I go to—my husband, who was very needy, or my child, who was also needy but in a different way?

The Balance of Caregiving

The experiences of individual families ground a discussion of caregiving across generations more viscerally than do any statistics. But what they alone cannot do is answer certain key questions: How common is it for working adults not to receive help from their own parents? How often do working Americans need to provide help to their parents, spouses, partners, or other family members as well as to their children? To answer these questions, a representative sample of more than three thousand adults from across the country were asked how much time they spent giving assistance to and receiving assistance from family members in the previous month (see Appendix B, The Survey of Midlife in the United States [MIDUS]).

The results of our analyses make clear how few Americans do or can rely on grandparents for assistance in meeting child-care or other work and family needs. Nearly eight out of ten working parents reported that they had received no unpaid assistance from their parents in the previous month. Only one in ten reported that they had received eight or more hours of assistance in the previous month (see Figure 5.1). It was more common for working Americans to be assisting their own parents. Nearly four out of ten working Americans were providing unpaid assistance to their own parents; half of these were providing the equivalent of one or more day a month (see Figure 5.2). When emotional support was included as assistance, seven out of ten working Americans provided support to their parents each month; half of these provided one or more days a month of support. One in ten working Americans provided forty or more hours of unpaid assistance and emotional support each month.

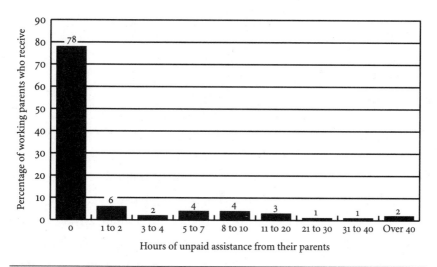

FIGURE 5.1   How Much Unpaid Assistance Do Working Adults Receive from Their Parents Each Month?

NOTE: The figure is based on data we collected in the Survey of Midlife in the United States.

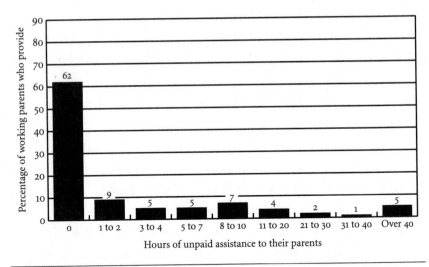

FIGURE 5.2   How Much Unpaid Assistance Do Working Americans Provide to Their Parents Each Month?

NOTE: The figure is based on data we collected in the Survey of Midlife in the United States.

An Outdated National Response

The needs of the elderly have garnered more than a passing response from American politicians. Unlike children, the elderly can vote. Whether because they have more time, fewer conflicting work and family obligations, or greater commitment, the elderly vote in larger numbers than do younger and middle-aged working adults. Although older Americans accounted for slightly less than 13 percent of the population in 1990 (as noted earlier), they accounted for 22 percent of those voting.[12] In fact, in each of the past three presidential elections, those 65 and over have voted at higher rates than any other age group.[13]

Government responses to the needs of an aging population have been significant and sustained. Congress passed Social Security legislation in 1935 to guarantee a retirement income to the elderly and Medicare in 1965 to provide medical insurance for the elderly. Unlike the related programs of welfare and Medicaid, which provide income and health insurance for families living in poverty, Social Security and Medicare were designed to cover all older citizens, regardless of income. While welfare and Medicaid have come under attack, Medicare and Social Security have proven nearly invulnerable politically.

Social Security sought to address a problem that was new early in the twentieth century: the retirement of men who, with their families, had relied completely on income from work in the industrial labor force to survive. In the nineteenth century, when the majority of adults lived and worked on farmland, families could rely on their farms for food. In the twentieth century, after the majority of men moved into the industrial labor force, families depended upon wages to pay for necessities. When the men who were being relied upon for wages grew too old to stay at their jobs, many were left without other sources of consistent income. Social Security, together with private pensions and savings, began to fill this income gap.

Toward the close of the twentieth century, debate over the future of Social Security has heated up. The debate is neither over whether Social Security is necessary nor over whether Social Security meets all the needs of the elderly. Rather, the debate has focused almost entirely on how to keep Social Security solvent. Watching the aging of the population and the relative decline in the number of working-age adults for every retired American, policymakers and pundits alike have repeatedly asked how the relatively smaller proportion of workers in the future will be able to pay for the retirement of a higher proportion of elderly Americans. This problem may be overstated. Though the rise in the number of older men relative to the number of working-age men has been dramatic, the rise in the number of women in the paid labor force has been equally so and holds equally important implications for the lives of the elderly. If in the future, the gender gap is eliminated and women earn as much as men, then the projected solvency problems of Social Security will be markedly reduced.

However, with dramatically more men and women in the paid labor force, there will be significantly fewer adult children at home available to care for the health and daily needs of retired older Americans. While a great deal of attention has been paid to the change in the number of workers, practically no attention has been paid to this change in the number of caregivers. In the past, the majority of elder care has been unpaid and has been performed by family members. If left unaddressed, the new caregiving gap will have consequences for older individuals and families as serious as the consequences of previous income gaps. Who will care for the 86-year-old who cannot bathe himself or get up from the toilet alone? Who will care for the 93-year-old who cannot feed herself? This problem—already large—will grow rapidly as the number of older people in general rises, as the number of the oldest with the greatest caregiving needs markedly increases, and as the economic resources available to older individuals to pay for care decline due to limits placed on Social Security and to decreases in the private pension system (which Social Security was designed to complement but not replace).[14]

While the problems will be great for all older individuals, they will be most devastating for those who receive no government services and cannot afford to pay for help in their homes or to move to facilities where they would receive quality care. The number of elderly people living in poverty has declined significantly,[15] and has fallen below the number of children living in poverty, but millions of older Americans continue to live on very low incomes. One in three older women and one in five older men live at or near the poverty level.[16] Among the elderly poor, Social Security is frequently insufficient to get them out of poverty, much less to meet their health or other care needs. As a result of being linked to lifetime earnings, Social Security provides the least income in old age to those Americans who are most likely to need it: people whose low lifetime earnings made it difficult or impossible to set aside substantial savings for old age. As important an income source as Social Security is for older Americans, it provides less income than a number of programs in European countries that do not rely on the inequities of supplements from private pensions and investments to bring the elderly out of poverty.[17]

Health problems leading to a loss of income can easily send those near the poverty level below it. That is one reason why the elderly, as they age, become increasingly likely to experience poverty. Moreover, even when health problems do not lead to loss of income, they lead to increased expenses, which can make basic necessities unaffordable to those living near the poverty line. Finally, low-income older Americans live in greater risk because on average they have more disabilities, chronic health problems, and activity limitations than do higher-income older Americans, as well as fewer resources with which to get help for these problems.

Neither the federal government nor the states have responded adequately to older Americans' care needs. Round-the-clock care is available for some elderly people who are completely disabled and cannot take care of themselves—primarily the completely destitute who receive government assistance and the very wealthy. But for the majority of older Americans, such care is unavailable and unaffordable. Many low- and middle-income families have too much income to qualify for the meager services provided by the state and federal governments yet far too little to pay for care themselves. Not only is round-the-clock residential care unavailable to many, but the far smaller amounts of assistance critical for older people who live on their own are often unaffordable. In most of the country, if elderly people need help dressing or bathing but otherwise can care for themselves, they have no access to public assistance, even if they do not have any family members who can help.

The specific services available to the elderly vary from state to state for two reasons: First, states decide what services will be provided to the elderly under the federal Medicaid program. Second, each state decides whether or not to augment federally funded (and state-matched) services for nursing home care with state-provided supports such as home health aides to older people living at home. Some states are particularly bad. For example, Alabama has no state-funded programs to provide care for the elderly, and even under the federal Medicaid programs the state allows practically no services. Having difficulty eating, drinking, going to the bathroom, bathing, or dressing is not enough for even the poorest people to qualify for services. Only a sharply delimited set of medical needs and diagnoses such as those requiring major interventions like having a tracheostomy and using supplemental oxygen to breathe would qualify a person for services.[18] Likewise, Mississippi offers no state programs; to receive nursing facility services under Medicaid, an elderly person must have difficulty with not just one but several essential activities of daily living, such as eating, drinking, going to the bathroom, or bathing. Other states provide services, but only of a limited nature: Some help people with housing but not with meals; others help people who have dementia but not people who are simply too weak or frail to meet their own basic needs; and many set income eligibility criteria so low that few people are eligible. To receive state aid in Arkansas, a person must have less than $806 in monthly income; in Colorado, less than $860—about $200 a week. While that amount might enable some of those lucky enough to have paid-for homes to meet their other basic needs, it certainly would not be enough for disabled older Americans to cover the costs on their own of needing help with meal preparation, dressing, or bathing.

The United States has done no better at filling the gaps for older Americans who need unpredictable but urgent assistance. Even when such care or routine care is available, though, it cannot supplant the need for adult children to be with parents who are desperately ill or dying, to take leave from work to help an aging parent move into a nursing home, or to help in other ways when an older person's ability to meet his or her basic daily needs for food, clothing, or shelter is suddenly threatened. For the many older Americans who live far from their children and for those without children, a niece or a nephew or other extended-family member may be the only person available to help. Yet no public policies and only the rarest private ones allow extended-family members to provide this critical assistance while they are working.

As the twenty-first century begins—and the largest boom in older citizens in recorded history continues—the United States has only the FMLA, which requires only large employers to offer only a portion of employees the opportunity to take unpaid leave during the serious illness of a parent. As important a benefit as this is, it is like saying that providing one meal every other day for people who otherwise have no food is an adequate solution. The FMLA offers nowhere near enough to meet basic needs, since it covers only serious illnesses of parents and spouses while providing no coverage for grandparents, aunts, uncles, in-laws, or other close adult family members and provides only for unpaid leave that is unaffordable to many.

The holes in this safety net are far larger than the webbing the net is composed of. For example, if an elderly uncle with dementia gets lost wandering in the city streets and his niece urgently needs to find him, no unpaid leave is provided. If elder care falls through for a 78-year-old man who cannot feed himself, his son isn't assured unpaid leave to offer the basic care required. In fact, no meeting of essential daily needs is covered under the FMLA. Furthermore, as mentioned in previous chapters, tens of millions of working Americans are not covered at all by the FMLA, either because their employer is small or because they have been working for less than a year or for less than 1,250 hours. The unpaid nature of the FMLA leaves millions more only with unaffordable coverage. It should not be a surprise, then, for example, that in heat waves, a large number of elderly people in many cities across the country are seriously at risk, and some die, because no one is available to see that they drink enough liquids, have adequate ventilation, or are taken to a cooler location. Similar tragedies occur with each cold wave. These episodes serve as the canaries in the coal mine.

The Needs of the Majority

So where does that leave us? None of the simple stereotypes hold. Most working Americans do *not* have a grandparent or other extended family member available to help them address children's routine or unpredictable needs, as we found not only for the population as a whole but for every subgroup we examined. Often political debates about the conditions the working poor face have stereotyped single, low-income mothers as always having a grandmother available to help, but this is far from the case. Similarly, not all older Americans need assistance themselves with activities of daily living; the truth is far more complex and dynamic. The amount of assistance working Americans provide to their parents is similar to the amount of assistance they receive from their parents. In a majority of families, receiving help increases the sense of obligation to provide help when needed. So while the assistance received from grandparents lightens the caretaking burden at one point in time, it increases that same caretaking burden later on. As noted earlier, as adults move toward old-old age, they are far less likely to be able to help their children with caretaking and far more likely to need assistance themselves.

This more accurate picture of caregiving assistance and need across the life span has several important implications both for the care older Americans can provide and for the assistance they need to survive. First, only a small minority of grandparents are in a position to provide regular care for grandchildren whose parents are working. However, a significant minority of grandparents (and other extended family members) could help with the unpredictable health and developmental needs of grandchildren, nieces, and nephews more often and more extensively if public and private policy facilitated that assistance. This would be especially true for working grandparents and other relatives who needed leave from work to care for children in emergencies. Second, improving the quality and availability of routine elder care is as important for the rapidly growing number of older Americans, the majority of whom no longer have a family member available to provide full-time routine care, as it is for children. Third, even when elder care is available, older Americans will continue to need family members' assistance with emergency or unpredictable care, which working adults can provide adequately only if they have leave from or flexibility at work.

In sum, we as a nation must recognize that over the past 130 years, being a grandparent has changed as markedly as being a parent or a child. While our social institutions have adapted rapidly to the dramatic technological changes over the same period, they have barely begun to respond to the changes in working families. The critical dilemmas Americans of all generations are facing—both when they seek routine care and when unpredictable health and developmental problems arise—are far from being addressed adequately in public and private policies, community services, and civil institutions.

CHAPTER SIX

Economic Inequalities Magnified: Greater Strains, Fewer Resources

OVER THE PAST two decades, the United States has had considerably widening income inequalities, which have adversely affected middle-income as well as poor families. Moreover, when it comes to widening disparities in the conditions working Americans face, wages only begin to tell the story.

Low- and middle-income families face greater obstacles—at home, in their neighborhoods, in their children's child-care centers and schools, and at their work—than upper-income families do. When there is little state or national funding for preschool and school-age child care, communities must rely on local tax dollars and family contributions—with their resultant gross inequities. When our nation's school budgets are based on local property taxes, schools in low- and middle-income districts cannot afford to provide as many services as schools in high-income areas. In the absence of basic job benefits guaranteed by the government, lower-wage jobs bring with them less or no paid leave and flexibility, and fewer or no supports for employees who need to care for children and elderly parents. While the resources available to low- and middle-income families are less than those available to upper-income ones, the needs they have to address are greater. As income falls, the amount and severity of health problems among children and the elderly rise. These disparities are affecting a far broader range of families than we typically acknowledge in public policy debates.

Disparities Disadvantage Poor and Middle Class Families

Employees' marked disparities in working conditions disadvantage families across the income scale from middle-class to poor. In our studies, families in the bottom quartile of income were significantly more likely to lack paid sick leave, paid vacation leave, and flexibility than were families in the upper three quartiles of income. But even people who earn just above the median income were less likely than those in the top quartile of income to have either paid sick leave, paid vacation leave, or flexibility (see Figure 6.1) and were significantly less likely to have at least four weeks of combined paid sick and vacation leave. At the same time, they were more likely than those in the top quartile to have to work evenings or nights. Among employed parents, 20 percent of those in the lowest income quartile work evenings, compared to 14 and 13 percent of those in the middle quartiles and 7 percent of those in the highest quartile; for night work, the respective figures are 10, 9 (for both middle quartiles), and 6 percent.

As demonstrated earlier, paid leave and flexibility at work can make a critical difference in the feasibility of a worker meeting family members' needs while succeeding at, or least surviving on, a job. People who can choose when to take a break can more readily meet with teachers about a child's school problems or with nurses about sick parents. Those allowed to select work hours have a better chance of minimiz-

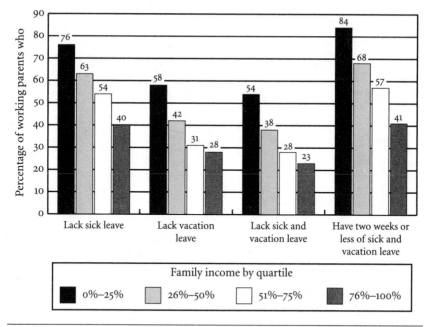

FIGURE 6.1   Lack of Basic Fringe Benefits

NOTE: The figure is based on analyses we conducted with data from the National Longitudinal Survey of Youth. Bars represent parents who lacked benefits some or all of the time they worked between 1990 and 1996 (1996 data were the most recent available at the time of this study).

ing the possibility that their young children will need to be left home alone before or after school. Those allowed to work at home can help disabled family members with eating or toileting. Those who can take days off do not have to leave their sick children by themselves. In each of these critical aspects of working conditions, the middle-income employees we studied were worse off than higher-income ones (see Figure 6.2). In fact, no matter how questions about flexibility and decision-making latitude were asked, middle-income working Americans and their families were significantly worse off (see Figure 6.3).

A gradient exists in need as well as in working conditions. For example, lower- and middle-income working adults spend substantially more time caring for elderly parents and parents-in-law (see Figures 6.4 and

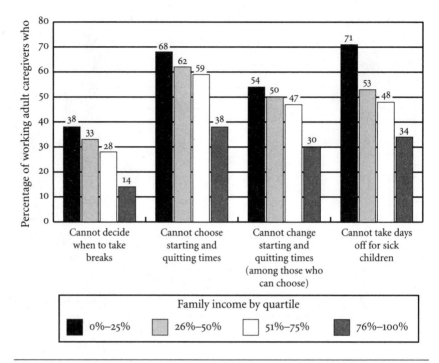

FIGURE 6.2   Job Inflexibility

NOTE: The figure is based on analyses we conducted with data from the National Survey of the Changing Workforce.

6.5). One of many reasons for this is that lower- and middle-income adults and children get sick more often and have more chronic conditions than upper-income adults and children. Yet fewer lower- and middle-income workers have the economic resources to pay for someone to help them care for family members with health problems while they work, and the government provides few public caregiving services.

Experiences of Parents Working in Poverty

While the income gradient has left middle-income families in substantially greater jeopardy than upper-income ones, the poor face the

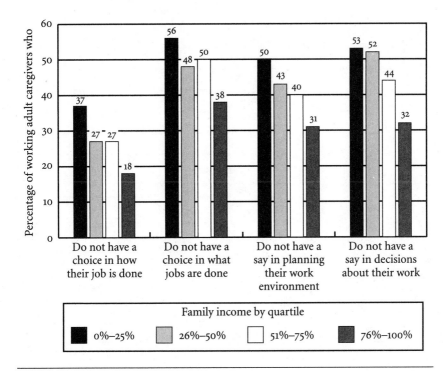

FIGURE 6.3   Lack of Decisionmaking Latitude

NOTE: The figure is based on data we collected in the Survey of Midlife in the United States.

worst conditions with the least resources to fill the chasms in services that threaten millions of families' health and welfare. When social institutions fail families, middle-income families have more resources of their own with which they can try, at least for a time, to plug some of the holes in the dike. While there is no doubt that families across the country, from every ethnic and racial group, middle-income as well as poor, are dramatically affected by the widening gap between American institutions and American working families, the poor are affected first and worst because they have both the most substantial problems and the most limited resources.

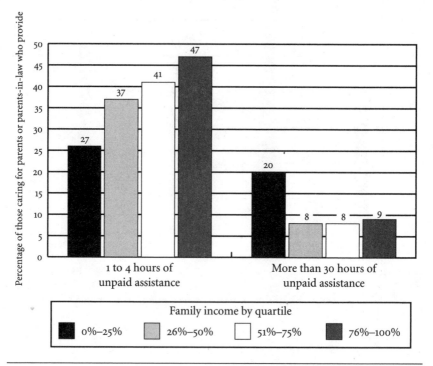

FIGURE 6.4   Time Spent Providing Unpaid Assistance to Parents or Parents-in-Law

NOTE: The figure is based on data we collected in the Survey of Midlife in the United States.

Stretched to the Limit: One Parent's Experience

Luis Marquez was one of these parents carrying the greatest burden with the least resources. A single low-income parent with few extended family members he could call on, he was raising two children on an inadequate hourly wage that forced him to work overtime and nights to get by. He had little time regularly with his children, 8-year-old Carlos and 5-year-old Yolanda, and less ability to take time off to meet unpredictable needs.

Luis sought to act responsibly in all of his interactions. His supervisor asked him to work overtime the day our first interview with him was scheduled. Since it was impossible to keep our appointment and to work overtime, Luis phoned the clinic where we had met him to say

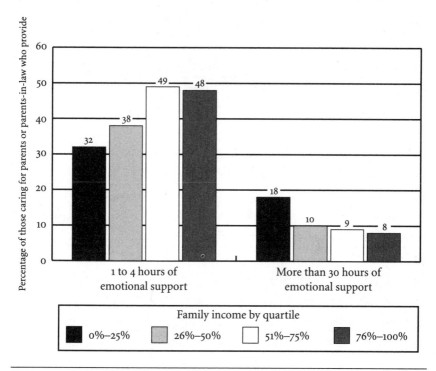

FIGURE 6.5   Time Spent Providing Emotional Support for Parents or Parents-in-Law

NOTE: The figure is based on data we collected in the Survey of Midlife in the United States.

he couldn't make the interview appointment. When he was unable to reach us, he asked friends to stay in his apartment to explain to us what had happened. He phoned his house at the time of the interview to reschedule the appointment. The day the second interview was scheduled, he was also called to work overtime, but he refused so he wouldn't miss the interview a second time. It was his birthday, and a cake from the supermarket lay unattended at one end of the kitchen table. He sat at a table in the clean, sparsely decorated public housing apartment with little furniture and no art.

Luis told us how he had become a single parent. Raised in the Dominican Republic by his mother, at age 17 he had come to the United States with his father, who shortly thereafter returned home because of advanced cancer. Not speaking English and totally on his own, Luis took the first job he could and got involved with a woman named Sylvia, with whom he eventually had two children. During their time together, Luis realized that Sylvia was taking drugs, and he struggled to help her get clean, even soliciting the support of her family. For a short time, Luis returned to the Dominican Republic because he had a chance to record music (one of his dreams) and make enough money to get his family out of the housing projects. But in regular phone calls with his family, he grew concerned about their well-being.

When Luis returned, Sylvia was on drugs again, and Carlos and Yolanda were poorly cared for. Feeling he had little choice, Luis sought custody of the children, then an infant and a toddler. Although the court awarded joint custody to Luis and Sylvia's mother, Luis raised them. When he received custody, he was just back from the Dominican Republic, did not have a job, and had difficulty finding one because he had limited English-speaking skills and less than a high school education. For a while, he and his family were on welfare, but he hated that. "It's like a habit. It's like a poisonous thing," he explained. "It's supposed to help, but it's not a help. It's something that keeps you down, I swear. You don't go [anywhere] on welfare." He went on to explain that when he was on welfare, there was never enough money and never the assistance he needed with child care or with training to get a job that would lift him out of poverty. The program's focus on single mothers rather than fathers affected his treatment.

After more than two years of searching, Luis found a job as a security guard. Barely able to pay his family's living costs on his wages, he considered food stamps. When he found that every three months he would have to miss work to go to an office to complete the paperwork, he decided to live with less to eat.

Luis wanted to visit his children's school regularly. But he couldn't afford to visit the school often, since each visit meant losing time from work, losing income, and having more trouble paying the bills. He described one visit when he watched children playing outside:

> And this bunch of kids, young boys, had this little girl—they were like between the ages of 5 and 6. They had this girl in the corner, and they were all spitting on her: spit, all over. And ... if you see the look on this girl, she was humiliated. And she looked, she would just let them do that! And I called the teacher, and I'm like, "Look what they're doing to her!" And she's talking to someone else. And I felt like doing something because ... I felt so bad for her.

During the year before we spoke with Luis, he changed from a daytime shift to a nighttime one. If he went without sleep, he could be at the school in an emergency during the day—if he didn't have to work overtime. But working at night made finding child care extremely difficult. He would talk to the child-care providers, and they would say, "The child care, it's going to be from this time to this time," and he would wonder, what happens if someone has to work at night? To continue working nights, he needed to find someone both to care for his children at night and to get them to school in the morning. Eventually he was able to pull things together, to make a patchwork quilt that would cover child care temporarily.

He kept the night shift because it paid an extra dollar an hour, and he worked overtime when the family needed more money. Otherwise, his pay didn't even cover the rent in public housing after he paid for the car he needed to get to work and for his children's child care, food, and clothing. Even with the overtime, he could afford the child care only because the child-care provider, who received income from welfare, accepted well below the minimum wage. Luis's situation was faced by many working poor parents, who rely on the only child care they can afford: child care that has been indirectly subsidized through welfare payments. Under welfare reform, Luis, his children, and the child-care provider would all be affected.

When asked whether he had any concerns about his children's health or development, Luis responded immediately with concerns about violence. He talked about kids in his neighborhood punching his daughter and sexually harassing her when she was barely out of kindergarten. He talked about not knowing how his son would respond to threats of violence. Seeing the child being spat on at Carlos's school made Luis think about his son:

> Maybe he [doesn't] want that kind of stuff to happen to him or whatever; he wants to make the other kids respect him. ... One day they called me and told me that he got in trouble. But he said, "Okay, Daddy, I was drinking water and this big kid came and pushed me because he wanted to drink first." ...What came through his mind is, ... I got to hit this guy for what he did.

Luis knew what he wanted to teach Carlos:

> He was saying to me that it's hard when someone else hits me and I can't hit him back; I just can't control myself. ... And I said, "...you do a lot of stuff that makes me—you, you make me lose control sometimes. Boy, if I would do that, I would be spanking you all day. So we all have to deal with that." This way he kind of smiles. He knew. He understood what I was saying. But I know what he's going through. You know, in school, kids go through a lot.

But Luis had only twenty or thirty minutes with Carlos on most days, and he worried that Carlos might become either a perpetrator or a victim of violence:

> It's like me myself: if ... I am walking down the street and I see trouble, I go the other way. ... I've been on occasions that I have been called a lot of

things, and I just had to walk away, but some people don't know how to deal with that. And I'm afraid that he might have an encounter like that one and won't know how to control himself. That's how you find trouble, and I just want him to know that either way—whether you defend yourself or whether you win or what—anyways, you're going to lose. And the best thing to do is just walk away.

When Carlos had just finished second grade and Yolanda had just finished kindergarten, Luis wanted their school to address the causes of violence as an integral part of the curriculum:

I'm worried about—and this is in the whole school system—that they only focus on violence on a special occasion. They should do it as a basic, like a routine every [day]: Okay, at two o'clock every day ... you got to talk about this. And they don't do that. It's like they don't pay much attention to that subject. And I've been talking about it to some people. By September I want to sit down and see if I can organize something. They gotta do something. They teach about plants and everything, you know. I think [teaching about avoiding violence is much] more important because people go through that every day.

Later he went on to say, "In a way, when you teach them about violence, you also teach about *respecting* people, all human beings, and [having] tolerance."

At the time of our interview, Luis was about to lose his job, the only one he had had since becoming solely responsible for his children. The security firm he worked for had lost its contract to provide security at the bank where he worked nights. "To tell you the truth, it don't look good. I don't know what I am going to do next month," he said. When asked what would happen if he didn't find another job, he simply responded, "I don't even want to think about it. I just, I am going to do my best for, to get a job ... anything." The woman who had been baby-sitting for his children was leaving and was not going to be available much longer. Luis knew all too well the struggles he would face finding another job and putting together another threadbare patchwork quilt of care for his children. And recognizing the bottom line, he concluded despondently, "If anything happens to me, it's going to happen to them."

Carrying More of the Caretaking Burden

With fewer resources, the working poor carry significantly more of the caretaking burden. In our research, 41 percent of mothers who have been on welfare for more than two years in the past and 32 percent of mothers who have been on welfare for two years or less have at least one child with a chronic condition whose health and developmental needs they must address, compared to 21 percent of mothers who have never been on welfare. Fourteen percent of working mothers who have been on welfare for more than two years in the past and 11 percent of working mothers who have been on welfare for two years or less have a child with asthma, compared to 7 percent of mothers who have never been on welfare.[1] In addition, 6 percent of low-income employees care for a disabled adult; 24 percent, for an elderly family member or friend.

And because the poor have few or no resources with which to pay for help, those who have disabled children and adult family members to care for must spend more time directly providing assistance. Among low-income workers we studied who were caring for a disabled child, 49 percent were devoting more than one working day per month to that care; 15 percent were spending more than the equivalent of a forty-hour workweek per month. Among those caring for a disabled adult, 45 percent were devoting more than the equivalent of one working day per month. And of those caring for the elderly, 47 percent were also doing so for the equivalent of one working day per month. In all of these cases, the poor had to spend more time caring for disabled family members and other dependents than did middle- and upper-income employees. We found that single parents with a high school education or less who are also living in poverty reported that work cutbacks for their children affected more than two weeks of work during a three-month period. This is five times greater than single parents with a high school degree or less who are not low-income earners.[2]

Confronting Daily Care Needs with Inadequate Resources

Luis Marquez was only one of the many low-income parents we interviewed who faced impassable barriers to finding reliable, affordable, reasonable-quality child care during the hours they work. The working poor are significantly less likely to have an employer who provides financial assistance for child care, directly or through pretax programs employees can contribute to, or even helps find child care through referrals. Fewer than one in ten have an employer who sponsors child care or provides the financial assistance for that care. (The poor are also significantly less likely to have employers who provide information about elder care; only one in six receive such assistance.)

Wendy Johnson, a single parent with three children, explained how few child-care choices she had. Sending her son to a child-care center whose quality was regulated would have cost more than half of her $357 weekly income. When asked what was the most difficult thing about child care, she responded, "It's the cost and the quality. ...People want two hundred and something dollars a week." She explained that her son with special needs went "to a woman's home day-care center during the day." Wendy added, "I don't like it, but it's the cheapest. And I have no choice." In many states the quality of home day care is less monitored and regulated than that of center-based care, and less education is required of child-care providers than of beauticians.[3] Center-based care, which costs more, is required to meet higher standards, to have more teachers per child and to meet more stringent safety, health, and developmental regulations. In 1995, half as many children living in low-income families as children in higher-income families attended center-based programs.[4]

The front porch of Katie O'Donnell's home in public housing was covered with Halloween ghosts and witches. In her sparsely decorated apartment, signs of a child were everywhere: a large indoor basketball hoop in the kitchen, a plate with half-eaten macaroni and cheese. Age 26, Katie had a 5-year-old son, Eric. For the first year and a half of Eric's life, Katie had raised him alone while working as an aide at a teen center. Katie was single, and at first Eric's father would have nothing to do with him.

Katie described the struggles she had faced when Eric was an infant. At that time, Katie got her paycheck every Friday. Her coworkers sat together and talked about what they were going to do with their earnings. For a treat, on some Fridays, her coworkers went out to lunch together, but Katie stopped joining them. Instead, when she got her check, she would just cry. The first $150 of her $210 take-home pay had to go to a baby-sitter, who had no sliding fee scale. "Day care was really what stopped me from being able to provide for me and Eric, at the time," she explained. She just couldn't make ends meet. In debt, she waited for her tax refunds to pay off some of her bills. Katie explained, "I was making that right amount of money that stopped me from being able to afford day care and to afford living. It was one of those situations where I knew there was no other way for me to do it but get a roommate." But sharing housing still was not enough for her to make ends meet. Since she was making too much money to receive any of the limited government help available to working poor parents for child care or housing costs, but too little money to live on, she eventually left her job to go back on welfare and go back to school (when welfare regulations still allowed people to go to school without a two-year time limit). She hoped that with more training she could earn a higher wage and be better able to afford food, housing, and clothes after paying for child care.

Similarly, Brigette Fede, a single mother of three young children, could not make ends meet on the take-home pay of $170 a week she earned by taking care of elderly people in their homes. She explained, "I went to work when [the twins] were about six weeks old. …It was very hard. At that time, I hired a baby-sitter to come home. It was $125 for the twins; and my daughter, I paid $40 for. She was young, too. But I didn't do that for too long because I couldn't make it."

The problems the poor face in finding affordable child care don't end with preschool. When out-of-school care was unaffordable, some parents had to leave their children home alone, some turned to barely supervised settings, and some took their children to work. Ginny Harris, a home health aide, picked up her three school-age daughters and a school-age nephew in the afternoon and took them to work with her. She explained, "If you have to pay day care, it kills you." Unable to afford after-school child care, she said, "There's a program at school that's $45 a week. But if you multiply it by four, forget about it."

Mona Valentin, the single mother of a 9-year-old and a 6-year-old (see Chapter 5), described what it was like when she had to pull her children out of an after-school program she could no longer afford:

Every day I used to be on the streets, "Can they stay there? Can they stay here?" which got me very upset. What happened is [the after-school care] kept on raising the fee … figuring that I have enough to pay for it. They don't know. They go by your gross income. But after you get the little that you get from that gross income, that net income, you have so many things to do with it as a single parent. You have the rent. You have food. …You have nothing coming to you.

She explained further, "I get paid every two weeks. So when I get paid, that first check [each month went] right to the after-school [care]. My second check ... What I get, that net pay that I get, pays for my rent." After paying for after-school care and rent, there was not enough left to meet other basic needs such as food and clothing adequately.

Carolyn Storr, a single parent, lived in a crowded apartment with her 12-year-old and 8-year-old children. She was ready to leave her 12-year-old on her own, but not her 8-year-old son, Eric. So she sent her children to a barely supervised community center; it was what she could afford on the low wages she earned as a homemaker for the elderly: "Eric needs to be somewhere every day—[be] picked up and brought somewhere. So it isn't much of a choice where he goes; he has to go somewhere, whether I like it or not. I would rather something, [pause] I'm looking for something I can afford. This is the only thing I can afford. So basically, I take it or I'll have nothing." Carolyn had been unable to get her son into a public after-school program with a sliding fee scale because the number of parents who wanted to send children to the public program far outstripped the number of places available.

As noted in earlier chapters, young children are often left in the care of other young children, even during the evening. Our research using national data revealed that 25 percent of low-income families at times had to work evenings; and 11 percent, nights. Nineteen percent were on irregular schedules at some time. When older siblings were the primary caretakers of their younger brothers and sisters, rather than just occasional baby-sitters, all of the children were affected. Carol Grant, a low-income divorced mother of three, worked at a department store. Her 11-year-old son, Joe, spent the evenings caring for his two younger siblings, 10-year-old Sandra and 6-year-old Melvin. Carol explained what the evenings were like:

I had to work 'til nine. ... I had to make food, and Joe had to go and warm the food up. He had to help Melvin ... with his homework [and] sometimes Sandra. Then they had to do their chores and clean the house. He had to make sure Melvin was going to bed. And then I found he was yelling at them. Melvin would cry a lot. ...There's no supervision there, so of course he'd be like yelling like he's the boss and telling them what to do, or being, he was technically sort of kind of raising my kids. He's 11 years old, and he's raising his brother and sister. I wasn't there enough. ... I could see it, how he would torture Melvin and tease him all the time, and things like that. I could see it. It started to affect Melvin and the way he treated other people.

At 11 years old, who could blame Joe for finding the responsibility too much? He yelled at his brother and sister when he didn't know how to raise them or himself.

Idele Antoine, the single mother of 9-year-old Didi, explained that the after-school program at her daughter's public school ran only through fourth grade. When asked what she would do when Didi got to fifth grade, Idele explained, "Shut her up in the home. I'm preparing her now, as it is. I gave her a key. ...I don't have no other way." Idele wanted to change her work hours—for instance, from eight to four instead of nine to five—so Didi would only have to be home alone for an hour and a half and so she could "ease" her daughter into being alone. "I'm kind of nervous. But there's no way that I could [change my hours]. The office doesn't begin at eight o'clock. It's nine to five." Didi's vulnerabilities became clear as Idele explained how she was trying to prepare her daughter for being alone:

Anybody could trick her. I'm teaching her how to run the appliances and things like that. Well, she's known how to do the microwave and things like that. But the toaster, you know—things she has to plug in—it's what you have to teach someone. Remember not to touch anything wet. You know when they sit and play in the mirror with the hair dryers, there's a lot of things ... you have to think about if she's by herself. And I'd rather be there. It's not like I don't trust her. ... I'm worried about somebody else. ... I'm worried about how ... she's sociable and she cares about people. She would listen to somebody's story and fall right into it, and just, she'd never make it home. And I'd just like to be there for her, you know, a little while since, I don't know, just to help her along, because eventually she is going to be left on her own.

In the absence of universally available early-childhood education, low-income families spend a far higher percentage of their income getting far-less-adequate care for their children. According to U.S. Bureau of the Census figures, weekly child-care costs amount to 6.6 percent of family income on average. These costs vary little by race, with whites spending 6.7 percent of their family income on weekly child-care expenditures; blacks, 6.6 percent; and Hispanics, 7.1 percent. However, they vary markedly by income. Families who are not poor spend 6.3 percent of their weekly income on child care. But families with incomes between 100 and 125 percent of the poverty level spend 16.3 percent of their income on child care, and families living below the poverty level spend 25 percent of their weekly income, on average, on child care.[5]

The marked disadvantages poor parents face as they seek to provide routine care for their children go well beyond finding preschool and school-age child care. Even when these parents manage to find such care, they face enormous barriers because of the limited services provided. As many of the low-income parents we interviewed sadly commented, they often had no choice but to accept low-quality child care; it was all they could afford. Because poor families must spend a higher percentage of their sparse income on child care, they can rarely afford accredited, high-quality early-childhood education. They are far more likely to have their children in nonregulated settings, half of which, according to the Child Care Bureau, offer inadequate care.[6] As our national Daily Diaries Study demonstrated, low-income parents are also more likely to have to interrupt work because of problems with their child care (see Chapter 2).

Parents living in poverty and their children frequently deal with underresourced schools as well. The fewer resources schools have, the greater the burden placed on parents to fill educational gaps if their children are to have any chance in a labor market where opportunities are driven by educational outcomes. The limited availability of textbooks and computers in many poor schools provides just one example of how the lack of materials affects the daily lives of schoolchildren and parents. In well-financed schools, children are given current textbooks to take home. Many middle- and upper-class families also have Internet access at home, and the children can use supplemental online sources when writing reports and completing other assignments. In underfinanced schools, the textbooks that are available can be twenty years old yet treated like invaluable treasures because the schools do not have the twenty or thirty dollars per child needed to buy new books. Furthermore, because of the limited budgets, children are not allowed to take home even these outdated textbooks, which could not be replaced if lost. To enable their children to study, poor parents often must use time outside of work hours to help find contemporary educational resources essential for their children's study, competition, and advancement. As it is, equal opportunity is a meaningless phrase for all too many of our children.

Facing Unpredictable Demands with Poor Working Conditions

Poverty limits the ability of parents to meet the unpredictable demands children make when they are sick or have problems in school as well as to address the routine demands of child care and school. Luis

Marquez's children, like many others in child care, were sick often when they were young. Colds led to ear infections, which led to Luis being called at work. Each time he left work, he had to take leave without pay, since he had no paid sick days, vacation leave, or personal days. Each time he left, he also feared it would reflect on his job performance and affect whether his boss wanted to keep him. "I had to be very clear with my boss and explain everything. It's hard, I know, for people to know about your business, but he had to know because otherwise he will think that I am doing it on purpose or something." When his children had holidays off from school, he also had to miss work without pay, since there was no one else to care for them.

Higher-income families can afford to take unpaid leave from work at times when poor families cannot. Studies of nationally available unpaid family medical leave to care for seriously ill children have documented how rarely low-income families can afford to take unpaid leave.[7] Higher-income parents also can afford to pay for substitute care when their children are sick and they must go to work, whereas low-wage workers commonly cannot.

For people earning barely above the minimum wage, taking unpaid leave to care for sick children poses about the same financial problem as paying someone else even the minimum wage to provide that care. Because these options are equally unaffordable for families living in poverty, working at a job with paid leave is particularly critical. As noted earlier, however, our research revealed that these parents were the least likely to have paid leave, and among those who did receive paid sick or vacation leave, low-income working parents were significantly more likely than higher-income ones to have one week or less of paid leave. More than 75 percent of poor parents lacked sick leave some of the time they worked, and 67 percent lacked paid vacation leave at some point over a five-year period (see Table D.1, Appendix D).

Lacking paid vacation leave as well as sick leave limited not only their ability to care for children who had special health or developmental needs but also their ability to provide routine supervision for their children during even a fraction of the days schools were closed. Yet poor parents were significantly more likely to lack paid vacation leave altogether or, at best, to have only a little. Eighty-six percent had one week or less of paid vacation leave, and 87 percent had two weeks or less of paid leave, even when sick days and vacation days were combined. Only one in twenty working poor parents consistently had at least four weeks of combined paid vacation and sick leave available each year. Three out of four working poor parents never had a job with that amount of combined sick and vacation leave over the course of five years.

Paid leave and flexible work schedules can be used as partial substitutes for each other when parents have to address their families' needs. However, low-income working parents have little chance to use either. Over the course of five years, 78 percent of low-income parents found themselves at times in jobs with no flexibility at all. Furthermore, among the people we studied nationally, low-income parents were significantly more likely to be at multiple jeopardy—lacking all paid leave and flexibility—than higher-income parents.

Low-income working parents were significantly less likely to be able to decide how their jobs were done and what jobs were done, to have a say in decisions about their work in general, and to have a say in planning their work environments. One in four working parents whose family income was at or below 150 percent of the poverty threshold lacked any say in general decisions about their work or in decisions about jobs to be done, and three out of ten lacked any say in planning their work environments (see Table D.2, Appendix D).

Parents with few benefits and little flexibility in the workplace may sometimes rely on other adults in the household to help meet children's needs. However, of parents living in poverty, only 6 percent live with a nonworking grandparent under 75 years old who might be able to help with child care. Moreover, low-income parents are significantly more likely to be at multiple jeopardy: single, with limited support, and without job benefits. In fact, 38 percent of low-income working mothers in our national studies were—at least some of the time they worked—single with no grandparents in their households and no paid leave (see Table D.3, Appendix D).

Parents who cannot take time themselves can occasionally rely on neighbors and friends. However, twice as many low-income working parents as higher-income parents said they could not rely on family or neighbors for help (since many of them were equally overburdened) and one and a half times as many could not get help and support from coworkers. Furthermore, low-income working parents were significantly more likely to lack both workplace flexibility and social supports. For example, four times as many low-income working parents as higher-income ones were in the lowest quartile of respondents in terms of both outside support and decisionmaking latitude at work (see Table D.4, Appendix D).

Significance

By any measure of equity, our nation's employer-based approach to meeting families' needs has failed. In fact, disparities in income are exacerbated by the dramatic disparities in working and social conditions that families at different points on the income gradient face. Because of our nation's failure to provide public services and set even minimal public standards for working conditions that affect families, lower-income families have a much smaller chance of simultaneously succeeding at work and caring well for family members than do middle-income ones, who in turn have a smaller chance than the well-to-do.

While economic factors help create the initial inequities, these differences are markedly exacerbated by the public policy decisions our nation has made, including, among others, our failure thus far to provide public preschool or early education to parallel public school, our failure to extend the school day and school year now that our economy is postindustrial rather than primarily agricultural, our failure to respond to the need for care of the rapidly expanding elderly population, and our failure to ensure employees basic family-related leaves from work. In most other industrialized nations, working families can count on publicly guaranteed parental leave; and in many, preschool child care or early-childhood education is already publicly provided. Furthermore, some nations mandate that employers provide a minimum number of vacation and sick leave days, while others provide public insurance guaranteeing paid leave for all families. These provisions limit what would otherwise be dangerous disparities across the social gradient. The United States does none of these. Consequently, as income levels decrease, U.S. working families face much steeper rises in the number of obstacles than do their counterparts in many European countries.

While it is essential to the well-being of middle-income families that solutions—namely, ensuring access to needed children's and family services and guaranteeing adequate working conditions—be universal, developing policy responses that cut across social class is even more critical to the welfare of low-income families. Throughout the twentieth century, our nation's approach to problems perceived as affecting only the poor has differed markedly from that taken toward problems recognized as affecting people of all social classes. It is well known that political and financial support for Medicare and Social Security—the universal health insurance and income-support programs for the elderly, which cut across social classes—has far outstripped that accorded to Medicaid and welfare programs targeted at the poor.

As essential as universal policies and programs developed for working families are, they will not eliminate the need for other programs designed to serve the poor. When existing poverty policies come under scrutiny, the ensuing debates must be informed by an understanding of the circumstances poor working families face. As our findings detailed in this chapter document, the working poor are clearly the worst off on every measure of resources available to them to meet their caretaking burden. The social and working conditions they face make it difficult for all—and impossible for many—to succeed at work while caring for their families, and these conditions jeopardize the welfare of children and adults who need care.

Understanding the extreme conditions working-poor families face is critical to our formulation of fair, realistic social policies. In 1935, when Aid to Dependent Children (ADC) was passed as part of the sweeping reforms of the New Deal, the country had decided that it was impossible for single mothers living in poverty, most of whom were single because of the death of or abandonment by a spouse, to support themselves economically and still care adequately for their children. By 1996, when Congress passed the Personal Responsibility and Work Opportunity Reconciliation Act and repealed the federal guarantee of income support for parents and children living in poverty, the country had made an about-face. A fundamental shift in the public debate had taken place: Instead of believing it was impossible for most single parents to care for their children adequately while earning enough money for subsistence, the public contended that nothing other than insufficient willpower was stopping single poor parents from working full-time and caring for their children well. The argument seemed simple: If middle-class mothers apparently could work and care for their children well, so could poor mothers. Little was said about the fact that there were two parts of the bargain: what parents contributed to the workforce and to their families, and what private and public resources were available to parents who were carrying out these multiple roles.

As documented in this chapter, the reality is far different. Low-income workers face measurably greater barriers to balancing work and the care of their families. In effect, we ask all parents except high-income ones to jump high—to clear a ten-foot-high bar. But middle-income families start at ground level, while low-income families are asked to jump just as high but are placed in a hole twenty feet deep in the ground. If we are going to expect all parents to be responsible in both realms, we must make doing so feasible for *all* families.

CHAPTER SEVEN

Gender Inequalities: At the Core Lies Our Failure to Address Working Families' Needs

NATIONALLY, debates about working women's experiences, discussions of how women are faring in terms of equality, and descriptions of the roles women play in the home all inevitably raise a series of questions: Do women play a different role in the workplace because that is the "natural order of things"? By choice? Because they are biologically destined to be the caregivers? Or because of socially constructed barriers?

Often these questions are answered with arguments that arise more out of preexisting biases and beliefs than out of any review of the evidence. Because it is important to understand how we got to the current gender inequities, which our national data will document, this chapter will start with a brief history of our nation on these issues instead of with the history of an individual.

Bans and Bars to Women at Work

It was not just in the Declaration of Independence that women did not get equal rights. Profound legal barriers to women's participation in economic and civic life existed throughout the first two centuries of U.S. history. Women's legal rights were restricted to a lower status in countless ways. In the 1800s, married women still could not own property, vote, start businesses, testify in court, or witness papers alone. When the suffrage movement finally led to women getting the vote in 1920, there were still more than a thousand state laws discriminating against them. In 1940, two decades after women received the vote and just before they would be asked to take over most of men's jobs during World War II, eleven states still legally barred women from keeping money they earned without their husbands' consent, twenty did not allow women to serve on juries, and sixteen did not allow married women to engage in legal contracts.[1]

It was neither by chance nor by choice that fewer women than men entered the U.S. labor force at the beginning of the twentieth century. Historically, both employers and organized labor worked against women's full and equal employment. In 1919, the Women's Bureau of the Department of Labor studied civil service hiring and found that the government excluded women from many jobs by barring them from taking three of the five civil service exams necessary to qualify for positions.[2] In 1928, more than 60 percent of school districts would not hire married women as teachers, and half would not allow women teachers who married to keep their jobs. The bulk of the school districts with a marriage ban had made their decision in strong economic times, but the percentage refusing to hire and keep on married women as teachers rose during the Depression. In private firms hiring office workers, bans on married women working were prevalent until after World War II. In 1940, half of insurance firms would not hire or retain married women, nearly three-quarters of banks would not hire them, and two-thirds of manufacturing or public utility firms would not hire them as office employees.[3]

But the barriers to women's work were not created solely by employers; the majority of organized labor leaders sanctioned the discrimination. Led by men who saw their role as protecting men's jobs only, most of the unions did nothing to eliminate the bans and bars against women—in fact, some favored them. They wanted to ensure that women, as a labor underclass, did not threaten either the jobs or the wages of men. In the nineteenth century, the constitutions of the majority of international unions prohibited women from joining.[4] In the early 1900s, the American Federation of Labor (AFL) newspaper, the *American Federationist*, continued to publish articles arguing against women's entrance into the paid labor force.[5] Even when women organized their own unions, the male-led federation of unions would often not let them join the federation. In 1921, the women's trade union league asked the AFL leaders if they would support women's unions in the ways they had supported blacks' separate organizations, but the president refused to do this for any "non-assimilable race."[6] Unions dominated by men became interested in organizing for women's higher wages only when they wanted to prevent employers from hiring more women, whose wages were lower than men's.

Bans, bars, and barriers were dropped slowly both in industry and labor. For most of the twentieth century, it was legal to segregate jobs by gender, and employers advertised in newspapers for men and for women to fill different jobs. Before the United States entered World War II, jobs for men advertised in the *Boston Sunday Globe*, for instance, included dentist, engineer, foreman, and salesman. Jobs for women advertised on the same day included maid, housekeeper, mother's helper, and nurse.[7] During World War II, record numbers of women entered the paid labor force when male workers were in short supply because of their entry into the military. Following the war, many women who had had wartime jobs lost them. Nonetheless, the environment for women finding jobs in the 1950s—whether due to the expanding economy, the decreased number of single women available to work, or other forces—was different. Firms previously unwilling to hire married women began to hire them if they did not have infants or young children.[8] Still, jobs remained highly segregated. In the summer of 1950, jobs advertised for men included sales manager, office manager, and general manager; jobs advertised one column over for women included bookkeeper, cashier, and salesgirl.[9] In the 1950s, the marriage bar was replaced with a pregnancy bar.

Most overt forms of job discrimination began to decline after the 1960s, when the practices were made illegal by the passage of the 1964 Civil Rights Act (at the last moment, gender was added to the list of prohibited forms of job discrimination). But in practice, there remained many jobs that few women had the opportunity to hold and many highly sex-segregated fields. Still, in 1970, the help-wanted ads included separate columns for men and women. In one week, the jobs advertised for men included business manager, office manager, city manager, and paid management trainee;[10] those advertised for women remained the lower-status, lower-paying positions of clerical personnel, secretary, and keypunch operator, among others.[11] While sex-segregated ads have ended, job segregation continues and women continue to earn significantly less than men and to have less chance of advancement in their jobs, as discussed later in this chapter. Now these conditions result from silent constraints on work opportunities rather than openly sanctioned discrimination on the basis of gender, marriage, and parenting. The interviews we conducted of employers, reported here and in Chapter 8, illuminate some of the ways women face disadvantage in the workplace and show how these disadvantages are inextricably tied to their caregiving roles.

Complex Web: Biases and Socially Constructed Barriers

Daniel Johnson ran the restaurant business his family had owned for generations. When we asked to speak to someone at his restaurant about experiences with employees, Daniel, as the owner and the person who knew the most about the restaurant, wanted to be the one. As he took and filled orders and addressed employee and customer concerns, Daniel described his business. Johnson's was a medium-size business—the size of many of the businesses across the country employing Americans. He had 135 employees. He was in the service sector, which is the largest growing sector in the U.S. economy. His employees are racially and ethnically diverse, and most have a high school education. When describing his ideal employees, Daniel said he wanted them to "be happy." He explained,

> Happy disposition is going to make for a better crew because we're really in the people business and in the entertainment business. Food is almost secondary because a great waitress can take an average meal and make an average meal really good. So people that have a good outlook on life are pretty important to me, in particular in the front of the house. Back of the house—it's nice for me to work with someone else that's happy also.

When asked to describe one of his best employees, Daniel immediately replied,

> The lady that just offered me a cup of coffee—she's standing over there. She's happy, clean, neat. Her demeanor is a positive attitude. You talk to her, she wants to serve you. Not that she's subservient, but that's just her own nature. And that's just a nice person to have to greet you and seat you. ...She's clean and neat about herself. ...There's a certain look that you want to have which is important. ...She's been here about twenty years.

And I don't have to tell her anything. She knows it. ...Customer came out of the bathroom one day and said she couldn't believe it. This [customer] went in there and after she washed her hands, [this employee] wiped the mirror, picked up all the papers on the floor and wiped the door handle. I'll never forget it. The woman takes pride in the place she works.

When asked to describe an employee who'd given him difficulties, Daniel immediately cited a man who had worked for him for "about four or five years as a dishwasher." Daniel said, "He just doesn't pay attention. Consistently needs to be managed and watched. He's always smoking. I don't know how he does it, but I have to work at walking as slow as he does." Daniel continued, "You always look to give him work, always watch to see what he's doing, and that's not the type of place I want to run."

Among Daniel's employees, the most common work disruptions involved their need to take off work time to care for family members' health needs. "Family—whether it be a child, a father, an aunt, a dog, a cat even—I think those are the most important," responded Daniel when asked what personal issues most affected his employees' work. Asked to describe employees who had particular family-care needs, Daniel first described the restaurant's chef, the father of premature twins. He noted that the chef went "right out the door ... every night to go see the kids in an incubator." When discussing his chef's situation, Daniel talked about how, with a workforce whose mean age is close to 40, "We have all of those issues of child rearing, family, etc., [because] most of the people in their late forties now have those issues." As Daniel was explaining individual employees' situations, it was clear he knew that caring for family members affected the work of both his male and female employees, even the men whose wives were at home and were the primary family caregivers. Daniel noted, for instance, "If the primary caregiver of the children is the wife and the wife is in the hospital, then [the men] have to be there, or find the mother, or drive here or there, and take care of all that."

Even though when talking about work-family issues he first named a man, and even though he named a woman when talking about individual employees who were outstanding and a man when talking about individual employees who were problematic, his perception of men's and women's relative responsibilities for caregiving discolored his views of women employees. When his comments were no longer about individuals but about generalities, he described everything through a gender lens:

> There's a male/female thing here, obviously. I don't think that men have as many issues as a woman does. ...Usually, if people's wives have had children, have had babies, they take about a week off or so—four or five days—and come back to work. The women that have had children seem to stay home much longer and have assured me that they're coming back and in many cases haven't. They've never returned in the same way they were before. I think it's a sexist thing to say, but a man that has a family can be more responsible now at work. The man tends to stay. It's that job security. A woman has ... they're just ...

Daniel paused as he spoke to a woman interviewer, but as he would later put it, he wanted to tell "the truth" and not "gloss it over." He continued, backing down a little from his generalization:

> The two or three that I have just never returned in the same level: (A) they don't want the level of responsibility and (B) the number of hours. All of them come back. One was my day manager—just never came back the same way. Works something like twenty-eight hours a week versus fifty-four; she has flex hours; her duties aren't as tough. She doesn't have what she used to have. ...I think in the old days if someone had kids, forget about it—never taken back.

Daniel didn't see never taking someone back as an option anymore, but he made it clear that he expected women's performance to be lower after a return to work and that he would reduce their level of responsibility.

Women are excluded from jobs and advancement by artificial criteria. When describing what he looked for in his employees, Daniel Johnson identified attitude and work habits, not number of hours worked per week. Daniel could have given more responsibility to the part-time employees he cited as among his best, but he chose not to. Daniel was not alone in reflecting biases. The experiences he had had with individuals—men affected by family responsibilities as well as women, outstanding women employees as well as poor-quality men employees—didn't alter his belief that women are less dedicated workers because they must meet their families' caregiving needs.

While part of his story was the story of bias, it was also more complex than that. While men do have significant work interruptions to care for family members, women continue to carry more of the caretaking burden in the United States. But stating that fact misses equally important points. To say that women are more likely to have work-family conflicts arise is equivalent to having said in the first half of the twentieth century, with segregated and deeply disadvantaged educational opportunities for African-Americans, that African-Americans had less formal education and therefore were less qualified for a particular job. Either statement has a portion of truth but misses the main point. In 1920, the lower level of formal education most African-Americans had was socially constructed. Because of racially segregated schools and because of the paucity of resources put into schools serving African-Americans, most African-Americans didn't have a chance to get the same level of formal education as white Americans. The same kind of inequity exists for women and work disruptions related to family.

Currently, employed caregivers have a high number of work disruptions because American society has not supported the care of children, the disabled, or the elderly. There is no universal access to preschool for 3- and 4-year-olds, as a number of European countries provide. There is no extended school day. At the same time, the circumstances women face are exacerbated by inequities in the home. Daniel noted that men were frequently calling women he employed to do the work of caregiving when they might have been available themselves. He described men's complicity: "As much as the husbands want their wives to work —when anything happens, Jesus, do they have to call? I always wonder, why can't the [man] do it?" Daniel simply registered frustration but continued to believe women will remain the primary family caregivers —and, therefore, less able workers.

In the final analysis, a series of factors were limiting the opportunities of the women Daniel Johnson employed. Workplace policies, their employer's attitudes, and lack of community and government supports for their caregiving responsibilities all exacerbated women's greater responsibilities for both caregiving and household chores.

Unequal Wages and Workplace Opportunities

Even though pregnancy and marriage bars and other forms of public discrimination have been made illegal, women remain effectively segregated by job and wage. In many ways, women are currently at as much of an economic disadvantage in the workforce as African-American men, which has not always been the case. At the beginning of the twentieth century, black Americans were worse off than whites. In 1939, blacks' earnings were worth 37 percent of whites' earnings,[12] and women's were more than 54 percent of men's.[13] But in the decades that followed, women's earnings relative to men's barely improved, while blacks' earnings relative to whites' more than doubled. In 1980, women were still earning only 60 percent as much as men, while black men were earning 85 percent as much as white men, after educational differences were taken into account.[14] In the 1990s, full-time, full-year-employed women still earned less than 75 percent of what men did.[15]

Currently, both women and racial and ethnic minorities remain at a significant disadvantage in wages compared to white men (see Appendix E). Various people have argued that this gender-related wage gap is not a cause for concern. They point to the fact that the wage disparities are not so great among young employees. However, while this is certainly the case, it is unfortunately not the cause for optimism that some wish. Rather, this largely reflects the fact that young women have not yet experienced the disadvantages associated with becoming care-givers. Among 30-year-old working women, for example, those who are not mothers earn 95 percent as much as men, whereas mothers earn 75 percent as much as men. Economic studies have shown that a majority of the pay gap between women and men is associated with their differing family responsibilities.[16] The gap is not merely due to differences in years of paid work experienced, to differences in the number of hours worked, or to differences in amount of education. In fact, when adjustments for education are made, the gender-based earnings gap—as compared to that between blacks and whites—grows even worse.[17]

While wages may be one of the most readily measurable ways that women's continuing workforce inequality is manifested, women's unequal position is demonstrated in many other ways. Research has shown that from the 1960s to 1980s, jobs were more markedly segre-gated by gender than by race,[18] reflecting the persistence of long-standing social and occupational inequities. At present, while some occupations are more markedly segregated by gender and others by race, the workforce remains substantially segregated by both. For example, in 1997, while 46 percent of the labor force was female, only 2 percent of carpenters, 6 percent of mechanical engineers, and 17 per-cent of dentists were female.

As alluded to earlier, occupational segregation by gender has occurred in the United States no more by chance than did such segregation by race. That these disparities are driven by social constraints—not natural interest or ability—and can change as the social constraints and values placed on occupations change is readily illustrated by historical changes in gender segregation. For instance, 98 percent of secretaries, stenographers, and typists are now women, although in the early 1900s these positions were filled primarily by men. While women have long been markedly underrepresented in some occupations, they are markedly overrepresented in others—principally those with lower pay, status, and benefits. While women account for disproportionately few of the relatively better paid university teachers, they account for 76 percent of the less well paid primary and secondary school teachers.[19]

More than in the past, job- and work-role segregation and disparities in wages and promotions are being driven not by explicit gender bars but by employers who, like Daniel Johnson, view men and women with caregiving responsibilities differently when hiring, rewarding, reprimanding, promoting, and firing employees.

Caregiving by Women:
A Disproportionately Large Load, Few Resources

In the national research we conducted, both working men and working women said that women not only have far more of the family caretaking responsibilities but also far more of the household chores (see Figure 7.1). More specifically, eight out of ten employed mothers and seven out of ten working women caring for their parents said they do far more of the household chores than their spouse or partner. Men agreed: More than five out of six said their wife or partner does most of the household chores. Similarly, women and men reported facing unequal demands from family members. Twice as many mothers as fathers said their family often makes demands of them. Working women are more likely than working men to also be caring for a child, for a spouse or partner with a disability, or for an elderly relative (see Figure 7.2). Those men who do help care for a disabled adult or elderly relative are more likely than women to spend one day or less a month providing that care. Women are three times as likely as men to have spent forty hours or more a month caring for a disabled child. Working women also spend more time providing both unpaid assistance and emotional support to their elderly parents or parents-in-law (see Figure 7.3). While our data make it clear that working women continue to carry a disproportionate amount of the caretaking load in families, they also highlight the share of working men who carry a demanding family-caretaking load.

While women bear more of the caregiving burden, they face worse working conditions than men. These working conditions often make it difficult or impossible for women to succeed to their full potential

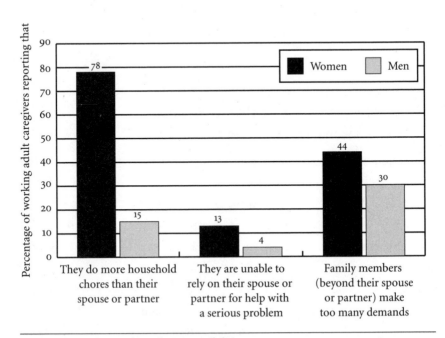

FIGURE 7.1   Balance of Family Responsibilities

NOTE: The figure is based on data we collected in the Survey of Midlife in the United States.

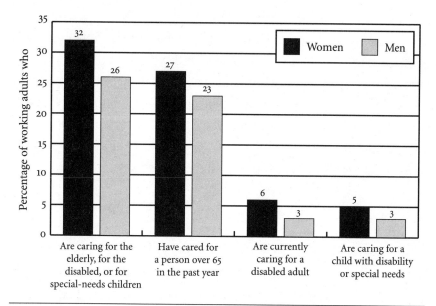

FIGURE 7.2   Caregiving Responsibilities

NOTE: The figure is based on analyses we conducted with data from the National Survey of the Changing Workforce.

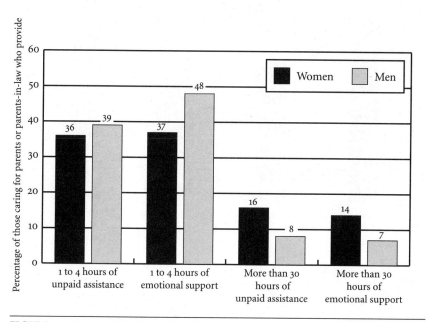

FIGURE 7.3   Extent of Caregiving for Parents or Parents-in-Law

NOTE: The figure is based on data we collected in the Survey of Midlife in the United States.

while caring for family members. Our national research revealed that
employed mothers were significantly less likely than fathers to have
paid leave they could take to care for family members (see Figure 7.4).
Not only did women have less paid leave in general, but they were less
likely to have choices about their work hours—when to start and end
work and when to take breaks (see Figure 7.5). In fact, on all measures
of job autonomy (such as having a say on what jobs are to be done),
women had less flexibility and decision-making authority than men.

Leaving a History of Inequality Behind

What must we do to eliminate these inequalities? Before discussing
possible future approaches, it is important to recognize that various

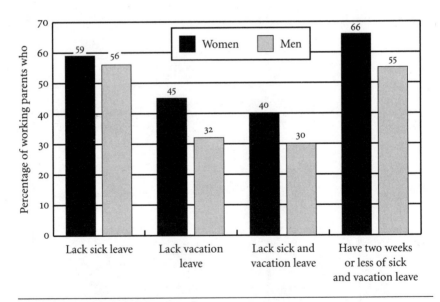

FIGURE 7.4   Lack Basic Fringe Benefits

NOTE: The figure is based on analyses we conducted with data from the National Longitudinal
Survey of Youth. Bars represent parents who lacked benefits some or all of the time they worked
between 1990 and 1996 (1996 data were the most recent available at the time of this study).

key approaches have already been tried—with limited success. Understanding the results of these efforts is critical to understanding which future policies are likely to succeed and which are likely to fail. Two broad approaches have been taken to gender inequalities in the United States over the past century and a half: working for an equal rights amendment for women, and developing individual policies and programs that benefit women. I recommend a third approach, for reasons that become clearer after a brief historical review.

For much of the twentieth century, the debate over how to improve the social and economic conditions faced by women focused on whether the best approach was special protective legislation targeted at women or an equal rights amendment. At the time of the industrial revolution, the work hours of paid men and women laborers reached

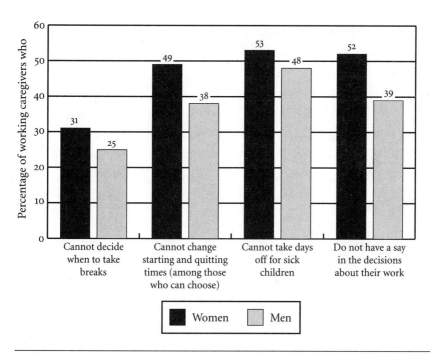

FIGURE 7.5   Job Inflexibility

NOTE: The figure is based on analyses we conducted with data from the National Survey of the Changing Workforce and the Survey of Midlife in the United States.

an all-time high of twelve or more hours a day.[20] And women, unlike men, were going from factories to homes where they put in more hours as laborers responsible for the households and children. Reformers worked hard to get minimum wage and maximum hour legislation passed. Although courts initially overturned labor laws that pertained to all workers, they let stand protective legislation targeting women. While not addressing the unequal labor burden at home, the legislation did help reduce women's total work hours.

While this legislation "protected" women from the worst abuses of a previously unregulated industrial revolution, it did not address women's unequal position both under the law and in most public and private institutions. To address this inequality, the National Women's Party submitted an equal rights amendment in 1923. The amendment was modeled on the Fourteenth Amendment, which had given African-American men equal rights under federal law, although it took nearly a century for those equal rights to be enforced and inequalities and discrimination clearly remain.[21]

Large political divides formed over the equal rights amendment, not only between women and men but among women who saw different paths as having the better chance of improving the social conditions women faced. Profoundly concerned with women's social conditions, well-known women such as Mary Anderson, a labor leader and the first head of the Women's Bureau at the Department of Labor, and Eleanor Roosevelt raised concerns that passing the equal rights amendment could threaten labor legislation protecting women.[22] They were concerned that such legislation would be struck down by the nation's courts if an equal rights amendment was passed. The equal rights debate continued throughout much of the twentieth century. The amendment won a majority of Senate votes, but not the two-thirds necessary for passage before ratification by the states, in 1946; two-thirds of the Senate votes in 1972; and approval in thirty-five of the states, but not the requisite thirty-eight, by 1982.[23]

Time made abundantly clear the limitations of special protective legislation targeted at women. The fundamental flaw with special legislation was that inequalities could not be eliminated with policies that solidified assumptions about unequal roles and responsibilities in law. Not only did concerns about special legislation prevent needed equal rights legislation from passing, but they hardened, rather than dissolved, the inequities in family responsibilities that underlay a great deal of women's inequality in the workplace.

What, then, should we do instead of creating special legislation targeted at women? Equal rights need to be guaranteed. There is no justification for half of the American population's having either fewer or more rights before the law because of their gender. Past proposers of equal rights legislation were correct: Eliminating one discriminatory law and one discriminatory practice at a time will allow injustices to continue for too long. But equal rights legislation alone will not solve the inequalities in the workplace, because those are based in the current relationship between work, both paid labor and unpaid family labor, and the gender division of that work, both privately and publicly. Equal rights legislation addresses discrimination only in the public sphere—and even then succeeds only to a point. It will address neither the current disparities in family caretaking burdens nor the fact that those disparities contribute to women's lower wages and more-limited opportunities in the labor force. Addressing work-family issues effectively is critical to our ability to address the wage inequalities and job segregation described in this chapter.[24]

Efforts to eliminate gender inequalities without considering family-caretaking burdens have fallen short in many areas. Several examples reflect the limitations of our current approach. First, movements to advance women's educational opportunities have succeeded in dramatically boosting the number of women who graduate from college, graduate school, and professional school, but women graduates continue to have fewer work opportunities and earn less than men graduates. Second, although gender-based job discrimination was made illegal by the 1964 civil rights legislation, that effort has fallen far short of eradicating the marked inequalities in opportunity and advancement. For example, throughout the labor force, the highest-status and best-paid jobs have the fewest women. As a result, fewer of the decision-makers who shape the public and private policies are women. On the Fortune 500 companies' boards of directors, women hold only 11 percent of the seats. Those women who do sit on boards are less likely than men to sit on the committees directing corporations: 6 percent sit on executive committees, and 2 percent chair executive committees.[25] Women account for only 5 percent of the 2,248 corporate leaders—that is, chairpersons, vice-chairpersons, CEOs, chief operating officers, presidents, senior executive vice-presidents, or executive vice-presidents—at these companies.[26] Similarly, fewer women than men hold appointed or elected public decisionmaking positions. Those women who are elected hold, in general, less-powerful offices that require less campaign money to win. Women account for 23 percent of state legislators, 13 percent of congressional representatives, and 9 percent of senators.[27]

As our own and others' national research has made clear,[28] to address women's inequality in the workforce we must address the inequalities in how family burdens and responsibilities are borne, because these underpin so much of occupational segregation, differential advancement within occupations, and differential earnings. In terms of specific policies, we need policies that make it possible for both women and men to succeed at work while caring for family members. Making this possible for women will remove many of the current barriers they face to decent wages and advancement. Making this possible for men is a necessary first step toward increasing the number of men who are willing to share family labor responsibilities equally with women.

Program and policy initiatives that support caregivers' ability to succeed at work are central to any agenda concerned with equality. They are central not only to decreasing gender inequities but to addressing class inequalities, since more women than men, in every age group of adults, live in poverty,[29] and the majority of these women have significant caregiving responsibilities. As noted in Chapter 6, working adults in poor families face, on the whole, far more work-family difficulties than their counterparts who have more resources, and they, their children, and the other family members for whom they are caring experience more health problems, school problems, and stresses of various types.

Even if one were concerned only with women's inequality, it would be essential to implement work-family programs and policies for both men and women. But there are other reasons to implement these programs and policies on a gender-neutral basis: They affect the ability of all workers to balance work and family and consequently affect our society's future. The welfare of Luis Marquez's children would be affected by these policies as markedly as would the welfare of Nancy McAllister's children. Nationally, nine out of ten single parents are women, but single parents such as Luis Marquez (see Chapter 6) also face horrendous odds. With no money for child care, no publicly provided child care available, and no family living nearby who could help, Luis found that caring for his two young children intractably hindered his search for a job. "When you don't have anybody … ," he explained, "you can't even go anywhere without taking the kids. And it's hard to be pushing the stroller and holding a baby in your hands at the same time everywhere you go," particularly when the places he was going were to companies where he was asking for a job. In some two-parent families, as well, men share in caregiving far more than is generally true nationwide. But at present, men are penalized at work when they share more equally in caregiving at home. Martin Amit was a 22-year-old cook who was one of a number of people we interviewed who was penalized for taking care of his family. When his wife's young daughter, Hannah, had a suddenly elevated fever, Martin had the only car available to take her to the emergency room. Being responsible, he called his workplace and explained why he would be late, but the supervisor said his reason was unacceptable. Martin was told that the incident would be written up and that he would lose his job if it happened again. The same solutions that will make a difference for gender equality will make a difference for our nation's children.

Debates over supports for working families often disingenuously pit families in which all adults are in the paid labor force against families in which one parent is at home and not working for pay. However, such false dichotomies ignore the reality that such supports would benefit all types of families. When the focus of policy changes is on broadly facilitating caregiving, stay-at-home parents gain as well. For instance, if a child became seriously ill or had to be hospitalized, an employed parent could take sick leave to help the stay-at-home parent provide care for other young children who were also at home. Similarly, an employed adult might need to take leave to care for an elderly parent while the stay-at-home adult cared for their children. Furthermore, if early educational opportunities for 3- and 4-year-olds or enrichment programs after school for school-age children were universally available, stay-at-home parents could elect to have their children attend part-time for the social or academic opportunities and could more readily meet other responsibilities of their own. (The use of public preschool by stay-at-home parents is already occurring in countries such as France, where it is universally available).

In summary, while special legislation that addressed only women's needs to work and care for family members may have been a useful temporizing measure at the beginning of the twentieth century, it has little chance of bringing about gender equality. For all those living in our country to have equal opportunities, we need to develop policies based on men and women having equal opportunities in the workplace and at home. While guaranteeing equal rights under the law is an essential step in this process, it will not be enough. To achieve gender equity, the price women and men have to pay at work for carrying their fair share of the caregiving load at home must be reduced. The first steps in this process involve increasing community-based supports that help care for children and adults and eliminating unnecessary barriers at work. While the experience of other countries makes it clear that social supports for children and caregiving improve women's labor-force outcomes,[30] that experience also demonstrates that eliminating concrete barriers to working and caregiving will not, on its own, erad-icate gender disparities. Historically, in companies where employees know or sense that taking allowed family leave will lessen their chances of keeping their job or being promoted, fewer men have taken the fam-ily leave. Clearly, unspoken biases—ones expressed in practice rather than on paper, such as Daniel Johnson's—need to be addressed.

CHAPTER EIGHT

Society's Best Prospect:
An Equal Chance
for All Children and Adults

FAILING TO RESPOND to the past century and a half's change in work means that we are failing to meet the essential needs of children and adults in the United States. The gaps in caregiving do not exist because parents work or even because they work hard. The gaps are formed by social conditions that never adapted to the changes in where and how parents work. Our society—like any other society with a future—must continually reexamine how best to approach at least three essential issues: what values the society will uphold, how the work of the society will get done, and how future generations will be raised. The failure to address how working families' needs are met in the United States is affecting all three of these.

As our Daily Diaries Study demonstrated clearly, work is being disrupted for young, middle-aged, and older employees; for men and women; for whites, blacks, Latinos, and Asians; for parents and nonparents; and for married and single people. As both our national surveys and in-depth urban studies showed, our failure to address working families' needs is profoundly affecting the health, development, and education of children. It is also severely limiting the support available for adults with special health and daily care needs. Furthermore, anyone who decides to care for children or adults in need has less of a chance in the workforce because our country allows workplaces to have unnecessary barriers to their succeeding. When we differentiate not just by gender but by caregiving status, we deny women and men the same opportunities, underutilize many individuals' talents and energies, and send a message that neither women nor men would be wise to invest in caring for their children, parents, or other family members. We diminish the likelihood that adults will take the time to voluntarily provide the care our whole society depends on.

Addressing these problems cuts to the core of American values. From the beginning, efforts to address equal opportunity have been fundamental to our national identity, and they remain essential to our democracy's vibrancy. In the nineteenth century, for example, universal public education was initiated because people recognized that children's life chances are affected by how much education they get, that the welfare of all Americans depends on how our nation's children fare, and that public action was needed to ensure a real chance for all children. Our research has shown dangerous disparities in the opportunities young school-age children have—with some being able to spend the hours they need learning, studying, and growing, but with many left alone, with little adult support, or having to serve as the closest thing to an adult that other children have. The inequities do not stop there. Because of the working conditions they face, all too many parents cannot meet with their children's teachers, stay with their sick children, or help their children negotiate threats to their development or health. Thus, some of the most needy children are left without support, not because their parents do not want to provide it but because their parents do not have the working conditions necessary to meet their children's needs. Furthermore, enormous inequalities exist in the opportunities children have from birth through school age, since our society currently provides educational opportunities only for those 5 and older, for part of the day and part of the year.

If we do nothing, American children clearly will continue to have nothing like equal opportunities. It is as if our country were telling some children, "You can attend school for half the day and part of the year," while telling others, "You can have educational opportunities all day, year-round"; or saying to some, "You can have help with math, English, and science whenever you need it," and to others, "Whatever your problem, you can try to deal with it yourself—but if you fail, too bad."

Support for Change

If we were to believe television portrayals, we would conclude that adults have few work-family conflicts. Only 3 percent of adults in television series recognize any work-family conflicts over a two-week period.[1] In contrast, in our national survey, 30 percent experienced some conflict over the course of a week. On television, preschool and school-age children apparently rarely need any kind of child care; only 16 percent clearly have some child-care provider. In real life, the majority of children need such care. School-age children's child care is apparent for fewer than one in eight children on TV, whereas more than three out of four American children actually need it. Elder care is even less frequently shown on TV: Less than 2 percent of TV characters acknowledge having any elder-care responsibilities, and fewer than 1 percent are actually shown assisting adults in need.[2]

The fantasy life depicted on TV as representing adult norms is in fact nearer to the experience of corporate and political elites, most of whom either have a full-time stay-at-home spouse or the financial resources to easily fill the gaps when society fails to provide services.

Heads of corporations and political leaders also have far greater autonomy in their jobs than most other working adults do. While the TV fantasies may reflect the assumptions of public and corporate decisionmakers, they bear no resemblance to most Americans' experiences or views.

As noted throughout this book, the majority of working Americans are caring for children, elderly parents, or disabled family members. This holds true across race, ethnicity, gender, education, and income (see Appendix F). Yet most are harmed by their lack of needed supports. It should not come as a surprise, then, that the majority of Americans endorse social change. Seventy-four percent of Americans say the government should provide financial assistance to middle- and low-income families to help pay for child care. This support is widespread and includes a substantial majority of Republicans, Democrats, and independents.[3] Sixty-nine percent say they are very likely or extremely likely to vote in elections for candidates who support after-school programs. Ninety percent of parents favor giving employers tax incentives to encourage family-related policies such as flexible work hours or benefits for part-time workers, 79 percent favor allowing employees to take time off as recompense for overtime hours instead of receiving extra pay, and 71 percent favor allowing workers up to two weeks of unpaid leave per year in addition to their paid vacation.[4] Most parents not only want more time with their children but also want their children to have the benefit of more time at school; 75 percent favor keeping schools open longer hours for classes, homework, and after-school activities. More flexible adult work hours, extended children's school hours, and a longer academic year are favored by a significant majority of low- and middle-income Americans, men and women, whites and blacks.[5]

Eighty-four percent of Americans support "giving people 24 hours of unpaid leave per year to take family members to regular doctors' appointments or to meet with children's teachers,"[6] 79 percent support expanding the FMLA to ensure that it covers more small employers, and 77 percent support coverage for more part-time workers. When asked about the importance of a series of benefits, the majority of Americans thought it was very important that employees be able to take "time off from work to care for a parent, child or spouse who is ill, for a new baby, or to recover from [their] own serious illness," to take "time off from work to handle routine doctors' appointments for [themselves] or for someone in [their] family," to take "time off from work to meet with [their] children's teachers," to have "enough flexibility to adjust [their] work hours to meet [their] family's needs," and to receive "assistance in finding affordable and quality childcare or elder care."[7] While the majority felt these were important, most families reported that "finding time for both work and family responsibilities" had been getting harder over the previous five years. Obviously, most Americans do not see addressing working families' needs as a special-interest issue.

Jointly Meeting the Needs of Families and Workplaces

If we agree on the necessity of ensuring that the families of working Americans are cared for and that all American families have equal opportunities, what are our options? In theory, there are three: Families solving the problems on their own, workplaces taking responsibility for the gap, or our nation sharing responsibility for what the families are unable to address on their own and workplaces are unable, unwilling, or unlikely to resolve. In a nation that values the myth that individuals can solve all problems on their own,[8] and in a historical period when advocating individual responsibility is more popular politically than advocating social responsibility, it is important to begin by examining what families can do, should do, and cannot do on their own.

Clearly, there is no substitute for parents' active, voluntary commitment to devoting a large amount of energy and attention to their children. Nor will there ever be an adequate substitute for elderly people having adult children, nieces, or nephews willing and able to be actively involved in their care. Replacing families' caregiving efforts with government's would be prohibitively expensive and inevitably would lead to lower-quality care. It would give a new meaning to the term "nanny state." Yet saying all that in no way means that most adults by themselves can meet all the care needs of children and adults in their families while working. To expect this would be as unrealistic as to expect that most laborers could continue to grow their own food, raise their own sheep for wool, spin their own yarn, and make their own cloth. No matter how committed to their family, if working adults receive no leave from work and no flexibility, they cannot care adequately for family members when special needs arise. Furthermore, no matter how much low-wage earners value child care, most cannot afford quality preschool or school-age child care or elder care that is unsubsidized. As documented in Chapter 5, most working Americans cannot depend on their extended family to fill the gaps. In the majority of cases, parents either live too far away, work themselves, have other caretaking responsibilities, or are too sick to provide that care. Employed caregivers themselves can do a lot, and their involvement is critical; but they can play the role they need to only when they have the necessary working conditions and social supports.

As noted in previous chapters, the United States for the past several decades has turned to the second option—that is, to relying almost entirely on the voluntary initiatives of businesses. Both nonprofit organizations and the government have largely seen their role as cajoling companies to do better or applauding the small fraction of progressive private initiatives. In response, a few corporations have taken a leadership role in changing working conditions by providing a wide range of important family benefits, but the majority of employers have taken a backseat. As documented in this book, many people lack paid leave and work flexibility, and few receive any support from their employers with child or elder care. Employer-sponsored child care is available to only one in eight employees, and even programs that offer tax savings for those able to pay for their own child care (that is, primarily middle- and upper-class workers) are available to only three in ten people. Elder-care assistance is limited to referrals, and even referrals are provided to only one in four families. Magazines like *Working Mother* list the top one hundred family-friendly companies to work for, *Fortune* magazine has its own list of companies with good benefits, and various nonprofits and the U.S. Department of Labor highlight companies that have had good initiatives. Despite these efforts, we are failing to meet the needs of most American families, and the existing voluntary initiatives have disproportionately benefited the families with the greatest resources and the fewest needs, thus exacerbating existing inequalities.

We are the only industrialized country to engage in an experiment that is almost entirely private-sector based. While this experiment may have been worth attempting, it has clearly failed to provide work benefits to most Americans or to change basic social conditions. Not only is the amount of work-family benefits provided by private employers small, but there has been little growth in these benefits.[9] This is not entirely surprising. After all, no one could ever imagine companies being in the best position to address similarly important national needs. For example, our country has not relied on companies to provide an education for their employees' children. Making a strong public education available to all citizens is essential to the welfare of all democracies and thus has become a priority shared by many nations. We have recognized that providing public education is not closely related to the work of companies and thus would probably be poorly attended to and poorly funded, if done at all. Furthermore, leaving it to companies would likely lead to even greater inequalities than currently exist in the quality and quantity of education available to low-wage families compared to that available to high-wage ones. There would be frequent educational disruptions for children when parents changed jobs, and the education of children whose parents cobbled together several part-time jobs would at best be uncertain. Just as it doesn't make sense for companies to be responsible for the education of their employees' 12-year-old children, it doesn't make sense for them to be responsible for supporting the early education for 3- and 4-year-olds or extended school days or calendars for 10-year-olds.

As a country, we have not relied on businesses alone to provide safety measures in the absence of regulation. Instead, occupational health and safety regulations were developed to protect workers. Nor have we relied solely on businesses to guarantee an adequate income. Instead, minimum wage laws and the earned income tax credit were both passed to help ensure this. All of the basic steps our nation has taken to ensure family income and worker safety have relied on roles for both government and business. In part, this is because of a realistic recognition that businesses thrive or die based on the quality of the products they produce and their ability to sell them, not on the welfare of families. As a result, discussion about the welfare of families almost invariably has come second in corporations. Even private enterprises that seek to help their employees address these problems face real barriers to doing it on their own. An employer who allows employees to have enough time to care for children with serious health problems, when other employers don't, is likely to attract more employees who need that time off. While a company can afford to give an average group of employees the time off they need, it may not be able to afford to be the employer chosen by all those working in its community who need to take additional time off. Furthermore, whereas a company can afford to compete in its industry while offering good benefits if everyone has to play by the same rules, it might not be able to compete if it is the only one providing paid leave and flexibility.

All democracies agree that some things are the province of government while others are not. The question that remains is, should addressing the needs of working families be the province of government? If the problems could be solved adequately elsewhere, addressing these problems—no matter how essential—would not necessarily be the province of government. However, we have reviewed the other options. Families can do a great deal, but the conditions of work make it impossible for them to solve all the problems alone. And employers by themselves have not addressed family needs in this country, nor in any other country. Clearly, the government needs to play a role. But this fact does not mean that the government should take responsibility for everything.

What, then, should the government's role be? In the United States, Republicans, Democrats, and independents, supporters of a small government role and supporters of a large one, bring to every dilemma being addressed the question of what the government should enter into and what it should stay out of. Indeed, in any nation, this is a critical question. There are many areas in the work-family field that government should stay out of. Just as government has largely stayed out of who marries, so too it should stay out of who works. Just as government has stayed out of when married adults have children, so too it should stay out of when they work. Even if we, as individuals, believe certain work-family decisions are wiser than others, none of us wants to live in a country where fundamentally private decisions are regulated by the government.

Just as there are clear areas where we should all be able to agree the government needs to stay out, there are ones where we should be able to agree that the government could enter without infringing on any individual liberty. The government already provides for public education for 5- to 18-year-olds. It could provide for early education in the same way without changing the nature of government and without infringing in any way on individual liberties. Just as families can now choose to send their 5- to 18-year-old children to private school or to educate them at home, so families should be able to choose to send their 3-, 4-, and 5-year-olds to public or private preschools or to educate them at home. We should achieve the same expansion in universally available early education in the beginning of the twenty-first century as was achieved with high school education during the twentieth century. Just as there is no infringement on liberty or individual rights in extending the ages for which education covers children, neither is there any overextension of government in lengthening the school day and year. In fact, the school year has been expanded over the history of U.S. public education (see Figure G.1, Appendix G).

Similarly, just as we have been able to agree as a nation that it is reasonable for society to set minimum work standards regarding safety or wages, we should be able to agree that society can reasonably set minimum working conditions for families. Undoubtedly, we will debate how high those standards should be, just as we debate what the minimum wage should be. But we need to debate these issues.

While the case for a public role enabling families to meet their most critical needs could be made on the basis of how important it is to American families and our democracy, as well as how intransigent the problem is likely to be without public intervention, there is a third reason for a public role. At the beginning of the twentieth century, families bore the cost of children, but they also bore most of the benefits. Children began to labor early on farms and in homes, and their wages and services helped their family members, young and old. In contrast, when today's children begin working, they will, through their taxes (including Social Security and Medicare payments), be supporting other families financially, as well as practically, through their labor.[10] While the benefits of children have largely been made public, all the costs of caring for children have remained private.[11] At a minimum, we need to take away the social penalties faced by adults who try to work while investing in their children. We need to remove the artificial barriers to their being able to succeed at work while succeeding in contributing to a critical national resource: their children and ours.

Basic Benefits for Working Families

To date, the public sector has failed to address adequately the majority of American families' work-family needs. As noted in Chapter 2, the only federal legislation passed with respect to these needs has been the 1993 FMLA, which requires some employers to provide unpaid leave under limited circumstances. However, it fails to provide any coverage to nearly half of American workers because they work for small employers, have recently changed jobs, or work at multiple part-time jobs to make ends meet. Furthermore, among those covered in theory, people who cannot afford to take unpaid leave receive no coverage in practice. Moreover, the act provides no coverage for the common illnesses of young children that nonetheless require an adult present, nor does it provide any coverage for educational needs, no matter how great; together these make up the vast majority of children's unpredictable problems. Major illnesses, including terminal ones, of brothers and sisters, parents-in-law, and grandparents are among the many adult needs that remain entirely uncovered.

We need prompt public action because our failure to respond is exacting the highest price from those families least able to pay it. Children and adults living in poverty have more health problems than middle- and upper-income ones, as noted in previous chapters. Similarly, the need for parents to be involved in the education of children living in poverty is even greater than the already real need of parents of middle-income children to be involved in their education (see Chapter 6). While children in poor school districts desperately need help from their parents, their parents are more likely to be working multiple jobs, less likely to have any paid leave or flexibility in their jobs, less likely to have access to the transportation necessary to get from work to their children's school during lunch hours, more likely to be commuting hours every day on a complex web of buses, and more likely to be working during the after-school and evening hours. Ensuring that all parents have paid leave and flexibility will not address all the inequities, but ensuring that low- and middle-income parents have the same opportunity as upper-income ones to visit their children's schools, meet with teachers and specialists, help their children when educational difficulties arise, and be involved in the schools is a critical part of the answer.

Public action could take several forms. In theory, possible options range from legislation requiring businesses to provide minimum levels of paid leave and flexibility, just as a minimum wage is required, to public insurance that parallels unemployment or disability insurance but that is used to provide pay during family leave. In practice, for several important reasons we should ensure that basic family benefits like paid leave are not coupled to place of employment, as they would be if they were created by simple mandates on employers. First, when basic benefits are paid for entirely by employers, there is an economic incentive to discriminate. This problem has already been witnessed in the U.S. health sector as a result of health insurance being linked to place of employment. Small companies that are self-insuring face strong incentives not to hire employees who have high health-care expenses or whose family members do. Similarly, if employers alone bear the cost of their employees' paid leave, they will know they can lower their employee-replacement costs by hiring fewer adults who are likely to be taking that leave to care for children or sick parents.

Second, when benefits are linked to work, there is no adequate way to provide those benefits fairly to all involved. Again, the case of health insurance is instructive. Currently, employees often face a lengthy waiting period before their existing health conditions are covered by new insurance, and such a period is put in place so that individuals with preexisting conditions will not take a new job in order to immediately use better health-care benefits. Without a waiting period, employers who provide good benefits would attract a disproportionate number of employees who are costly to insure. With a waiting period, employees and their families who are not trying to take advantage of the system but who become sick shortly after changing jobs are often unfairly penalized. Coverage restrictions probably would apply to job-linked family benefits as well. For instance, employees might be required to be on the job for a certain number of months before parental leave was available. What then would happen to newborns whose parents were forced to switch jobs shortly before the babies' births? Frequently, employers have waiting periods before paid sick leave is available. What then happens when an employee (or family member) is critically ill within the first months at work?

Third, when family benefits are fully paid for by an individual employer, the nature of the benefits is far more likely to be determined solely by what best serves the workplace, not the family or society. Institutional care for employees' sick children, for instance, might make it easier for an employer to move ahead with projects, even if it is costly to the children's health (see Chapter 4). If the responsibility and cost rested with the employer, we might well see a continued rise in the types of benefits that enable employees to put in longer hours and have fewer absences, even though these might not be best for the employees or their families. Clearly, a judicious weighing of the needs of the workplace and of families is warranted; neither should be excluded from the balance. If our choices are based on public debate, it is more likely that the needs of both will be considered.

No Americans should have to neglect their close family members in order to keep a job or afford to live; to prevent this, universal family leave insurance must be made available. What unemployment insurance was to families in which there was one wage earner and one homemaker, family leave insurance is to families with no adult at home. Unemployment insurance protected families that relied on a single earner from the cost of losing that one income. Family leave insurance would ensure that dual-earner families who rely on both incomes to survive and single earners who have only their own income to rely on would not lose income when they needed to stay home to care for sick children, elderly parents, or disabled relatives or when they needed to address their children's basic educational issues. As noted earlier, we cannot rely on that leave being provided voluntarily by employers. In fact, the amount of paid leave provided by employers has fallen recently. In 1986, 70 percent of those working in medium and large private establishments were offered some paid sick leave, and 25 percent, paid personal leave. In 1997, only 56 percent were offered sick leave; 20 percent, personal leave.[12] The numbers are even lower for small private employers: In 1996, only 50 percent of those working for small private employers were offered paid sick leave; only 14 percent, personal leave.[13]

Improving How We Measure Work Quality

If addressing short-term work disruptions—by preventing the unnecessary ones and providing working adults with leave and flexibility to handle the important ones—is a crucial first step, the second step is to address how we organize work and measure quality performance. When interviewing employers, we found that many measured worker quality by attendance, "face time," and willingness to go without breaks—even when there was no clear correlation between those measures and the quality or quantity of work produced.

Paul Nicoli, for example, knew what he wanted when hiring someone. Like a lot of other employers we spoke with, he noted a certain attitude toward work, and he measured that attitude with a yardstick developed when most families had only one adult in the paid labor force outside the home. He described his criteria when considering new staff for the health management organization where he worked:

> I would look at attendance—you know, what has been their record in the past. You can't always get this information, but you can at least bring it up as an issue. Someone's attendance at school is going to be what their attendance is on the job, pretty much, if you used past behavior as kind of an indicator. ... I use a story about apple pickers: You could have two different apple pickers on your team. One person does great—when they're there, they pick more apples than anyone else. But they're only there four days in a [given] week, versus the other person, who doesn't pick as many apples but is there every day. If you look at who picked more apples at the end of the week, the slow but consistent person would win. So I get my point across with that.

There was no gray zone in Paul Nicoli's parable. It didn't seem to matter to him if the fast apple picker was twice as fast and missed only a few days a year. He made clear from the start how he would feel about employees who had to miss a day to care for their sick children or elderly parents: They simply would have no good way of compensating for the need to miss work. Paul had other criteria, too. He wanted to hire dependable, reliable people who were good at customer service, had plenty of job knowledge and expertise, and fit well into his company and the organizational culture. Yet he viewed these criteria as secondary to their never missing work. Similarly, John Davenport, who supervised people at a human services firm that employed more than a hundred people, began describing his ideal employee with "She's always there on time; she never misses a day." He added that this employee would have a great attitude and would work well with coworkers, so that everyone would "adore" her.

Phillip Brown, who worked for a heavy construction firm, expressed a common attitude when he said, "Most of the time we look for somebody who is willing to put in an inordinate amount of hours to get the job done." He explained:

> [The company is] generous to its employees in terms of pay. It's very cheap to its employees in terms of time; time's the only thing that's cheap. The expectation is that you will work hard, you will work long, and you will like what you do. It's a very difficult environment in some ways. Anybody who's not prepared to work a fifty-hour workweek will likely leave the company in the first year. Typically, a clerical works forty-five to sixty hours a week, and it's not a major league issue. If they do, they get rewarded. If they don't, they won't get rewarded, so they should leave. ...We had employees leave us because they had an issue with it at home that required them to be at home more than doing a good job would allow. ... I would tell you that if I had an issue at home that would require me to work only forty hours or less than forty hours, I would leave the company.

In an era of single-earner families, when all caregiving responsibilities fell on adults who were not in the workforce, such policies were a closer approximation of employees' commitment and drive. And nearly every employer we spoke with said attitude was one of the things they cared about most in their workers. With the radical changes in the labor force, however, these policies offer a poor measure of attitude. Even the smartest, fastest, most focused, most organized employees will still need, at times, to be late when their children's schools are closed for snow days and they have to make alternative arrangements, when their parents must be hospitalized, or when their infants have the flu. Even if they are willing to make up all the missed time, they will still miss some days at work. There will be employees who are less focused at work and make less of an effort but have a better attendance record. Promptness in arriving at the office will prove as poor a measure of quality output as promptness in arriving at a class would be of the ability of college students to write essays. It is an imprecise measure of attitude and a poor measure of productivity. Likewise, there will be outstanding employees who cannot routinely work sixty-hour weeks but who are willing to put in extra hours when the need arises and are able to get as much accomplished in forty hours as other employees in much longer hours.

Both employers and employees would benefit if success was measured by the quality of employees' work performance. In jobs that require a person to be physically present at specific hours on specific days in order to do the job well, attendance and promptness will remain critical for performance; but in many other jobs, employees' occasional shifting of hours or days to deal with emergencies would have little effect on the work. Similarly, while it is not possible to job-share all positions, some employers who are currently paying high salaries for long hours, as Phillip Brown was for clerical staff, could readily split the wages and the hours between two people—and again judge them by the quality and timeliness of their work.

Employers and employees alike are stuck when social conditions, policies, and programs have not changed alongside the workforce so that Americans can honor their commitment to both their families and their work. All employers need to know that their employees will reliably show up on time and be ready to perform at a high level, most of the time. No employers can get their work done well with employees who cannot be relied on. No for-profit or not-for-profit firm can thrive if employees constantly have to leave work because of inadequate child or elder care or because of schools or city offices or health services that have never recognized most Americans' participation in the paid labor force. But current social conditions make it difficult or impossible for many people to be equally committed to family and work. Those families who have exceptionally good social support networks or who have the financial resources to pay for—and the good fortune to find—family services are an exception. One of the most striking things about our interviews with families and employers was how often we heard the phrase "their family comes before work" or "their work comes before their family" and how rarely we heard anyone speak about the possibility of being profoundly committed to both.

Bringing Social Institutions into the Twenty-First Century

Just as employers and employees alike would benefit from an evaluation process focused on the quality and timeliness of employees' work rather than on family-related disruptions, so too would they all benefit from social changes designed to accommodate our national institutions to working families. Too often left out of any discussion of what needs to change so that both work and families can thrive are the myriad civic and social institutions whose practices are grounded, often for no better reason than habit, in the rhythms of a nineteenth-century agrarian economy or in the brief moment during the twentieth century when most households had only one adult in the paid labor force. There's not a business in America that did not take time out this year to think about whether its computer systems were Y2K compatible. How much better shape we would be in, if next year, every public and private office would spend the same amount of time to determine whether they are compatible with Y2K families. A few examples follow.

In the city in which we conducted the Urban Working Families Study, a parent needing to register a child for school had to go in person during the workday to the Parent Information Center, which had no evening or weekend hours. Making it possible for working parents to register a child for school by mail—just as they now can register to vote—or offering a wider range of registration times would mean that many parents could handle this vital responsibility without missing work. Similarly, as noted in Chapter 2, when children are required to get immunizations for school at pediatricians' offices and the offices open only during the workday, those immunizations require parents to miss work. If the same immunizations were given by pediatricians visiting the schools after parents had signed consent forms, parents would not need to miss work. Many private institutions have readily changed with the times. For example, malls are open in the evening, banks have weekend hours, and grocery stores are open seven days a week. But the gatekeepers for public services and supports for families are often available only between 9:00 A.M. and 5:00 P.M., or even for more limited hours, Monday through Friday.

Those providing public services to the poor require parents to arrive in person, more often than those—like the registry of motor vehicles—providing services across social classes and increasingly allowing services by phone, fax, or mail. One parent we interviewed who had just left welfare for work explained the difficulty with using a voucher program intended to pay for children's day care:

> They would want you to come in and recertify every two months. I just
> got a new job. ... How can you expect me to come in and see you every
> two months? It doesn't make any sense. If I came in before job hours, I'd
> be late for work. There was no way to come in after, because they close at
> five. ...They need to have some kind of ... a way either by mail or by fax
> [that] we could do this without having me have to leave my job.

As in other cases, the barriers are greatest, ironically, for the lowest-income families who most need child-care vouchers, food stamps, WIC,[14] and other public services and supports—and who are also the least likely to have flexible work schedules or paid leave they can take to go to public offices during the workday.

Adapting Work Schedules and Hours

We need to answer the question, how will working caregivers be able to meet with teachers and doctors, go to city offices, and carry out necessary tasks at other businesses and offices that are open only during the workday? There are two ways to resolve the dilemma: We can move increasingly to a public service sector that has evening and weekend hours, or we can increase the ability of caregivers to take time off during workdays. Currently, many American families have the worst of two worlds. Most of the private sector is moving toward a 24-hour economy, 7 days a week, 365 days a year. As a result, while a few choose nonday hours, many caregivers have to work evenings, nights, and weekends in spite of the lack of child care and other essential family services during those hours. Consequently, as detailed in Chapter 3, young children are being left home alone when parents have to leave early for work or arrive home late and no child care is available. School-age children are being particularly hard hit when parents' evening and night work means they have little time to supervise or assist with homework and other school-related activities. At the same time, most of the public sector remains on a nine-to-five or—as in the case of many school-related services—even shorter day. As a result, caregivers who are working weekdays have difficulty accessing basic public services and meeting with child- and elder-care providers, teachers, specialists, or agencies.

Where do we go from here? If we are going to accept the demands of current private sector work schedules—which result in many caregivers' having no choice but to regularly work evenings, nights, and weekends—then we need to ensure that quality child- and elder-care services are available and affordable during those hours. But there are alternatives to a twenty-four-hour economy. The United States has far more of a round-the-clock, year-round economy than many of its competitors. In Britain, for example, far fewer companies are open for business in person or by phone late in the evenings or at night. The U.S. public sector could decide to stick to daytime hours; at least then that sector's employees would not need to work evenings, nights, and weekends and could better care for their own school-age children. Companies could be encouraged through tax incentives or through wage laws to hire people for daytime work and to pay people more who had no choice but to work evenings and nights and consequently had to contract for care of family members during those hours.

How would U.S. families get their needs met, however, if adult members were working during the day, public services continued to be closed, and an increasing number of private businesses did not open in the evening and on weekends? One simple solution would be to move to a four-and-a-half-day workweek. Caregivers could then have their necessary meetings and set appointments during the half business day they had off and have the evenings to attend to their children's and families' needs. Moving toward fewer work hours is a realistic option. We have done it as a nation before: Reduced work hours were one of the primary goals and accomplishments of labor legislation in the beginning of the twentieth century.

Ensuring Preschoolers' Care and Education

While all social institutions need to adapt, the most important changes need to occur in our approach to early, elementary, and secondary education. Research on children who have the opportunity to attend preschool has shown that at age 6 these children have larger vocabularies and are better readers than their brothers and sisters who have not had an opportunity to attend preschool.[15] Children who attend preschool are less likely to need remedial education.[16] Model early-childhood programs have demonstrated a wide series of gains for children, including improved achievement test scores, a decreased need for special-education services, decreased rates of being held back in school, and higher rates of high school graduation.[17] Nevertheless, in spite of the well-documented importance of early-childhood education in how children fare in school, only half of all 3- and 4-year-olds have formal education. Early childhood education today looks a lot like access to high school education did in 1949 (see Figure G.2, Appendix G). In fact, the enrollment rates of 2- to 4-year-olds in kindergarten, nursery schools, and other preschools are lower in the United States than in thirteen European countries.

We can afford to do more. In the United States, public expenditures for early-childhood education are less than similar public expenditures in Finland, Norway, Austria, the United Kingdom, the Czech Republic, Germany, Italy, and Portugal. Our combined public and private expenditures on early-childhood education are a smaller percentage of gross domestic product (GDP) per capita than the public and private spending on early-childhood education in all the aforementioned countries, as well as in Canada, Denmark, Hungary, Sweden, Spain, Turkey, and the Netherlands.[18] State and federal governments currently provide so little funding to preschool child care that it is a parody of the need. Alabama spends $395 per poor child per year— even including the federal funding—which is less than a dollar and a half per day. California spends $536 per poor child—approximately half state funding and half federal funding—still only about two dollars per working day. These states are not exceptions. Florida spends less than $500 per poor child on child care and early-childhood development. And out of the $328 Mississippi spends, only seven dollars is provided by state and local funding.[19]

As a result, many families simply cannot afford preschool child care (as noted in Chapter 3). In over a dozen urban centers and states, the cost of having a 4-year-old in a child-care center is more than double the cost of public college tuition. For example, sending a 4-year-old to child care in Seattle, Washington, costs more than $6,000 per year, whereas college tuition at a public institution costs less than $3,000 per year. The more-than-doubled costs for a 4-year-old in comparison to a college student exist from Tucson to Anchorage; from Honolulu to Omaha; from Kansas City to Oklahoma City.[20] One option for low-income families is Head Start, the principal federal program aimed at providing disadvantaged children with early educational opportunities. But Head Start in its current form serves only a small fraction of the needs of children living in poverty. Only half of 3- and 4-year-olds who qualify for Head Start are able to attend at all. Due to limited funding and slots, the overwhelming majority of those who attend do so less than full-time and for only one year, even though most (as well as their families) would benefit from their attending more. The availability is even more limited for early Head Start, which is designed to serve those under 3 years old but reaches less than 2 percent of those eligible.[21]

Planning a Full School Day and Year

How we address the needs of elementary and secondary schoolchildren needs to change as markedly as how we address the needs of preschoolers, for a variety of reasons. Today, the most reasonable place for young school-age children to be at 3:30 in the afternoon is at a good school, but our society remains wedded to outmoded scheduling. There's nothing magical about the current short school day and 180-day school year. Over the past 130 years, the length of the school year has changed to adjust to the needs of families and children. As the materials children needed to learn in school for their economic survival increased, so too did the length of the school year. From 1870 to 1930, during a period of rapid industrialization, the length of the school year increased 30 percent, from 132 days to 173 days.[22] Then the expansion of public education stalled; from 1930 to the present, the school term has increased only from 173 days to 180 days.[23] However, since 1930 the availability of adults at home during the workday has markedly declined, and children have increasingly relied on schools for all of their formal education. Few children have a parent or grandparent at home in the afternoon to work with them on reading, writing, or mathematics. While extending the school calendar is long overdue, it will only serve children well if the quality of public education is high.

One result of our unresponsiveness to children's needs is that the United States is failing to compete in primary- and secondary-school education. Economists repeatedly make the argument that how individuals and families fare in a global economy increasingly depends on their educational attainment; and they, political scientists, and policymakers agree that the welfare of communities and nations will depend on the educational attainment of their citizens. But in international mathematics achievement tests, scores for U.S. eighth graders ranked behind, in rank order, those of students in Singapore, Japan, Korea, Hong Kong, Belgium (Flemish), the Czech Republic, Austria, Hungary, the Slovak Republic, Switzerland, France, Slovenia, Bulgaria, the Netherlands, the Russian Federation, Canada, Ireland, Belgium (French), Australia, Israel, Thailand, Sweden, Germany, New Zealand, and Norway.[24] Furthermore, the eighth-grade science scores of U.S. students ranked behind those of students in fifteen of the same countries tested.[25] Improving the quality and increasing the length of the school day and the school year would simultaneously provide more educational opportunities for children who need to be able to compete economically and help working parents who need their children to receive enrichment activities and quality supervision in a safe place. The use of existing school buildings would reduce the cost of after-school programs and increase their accessibility. However, most school districts currently send children home by 3:00 P.M., with no after-school care, despite abundant evidence that after-school programs produce a remarkable return on the investment.

A wide range of after-school programs has been shown to improve children's academic achievement across social class.[26] Studies have shown that children who participate in after-school programs not only spend more time on their homework but also are more likely to complete their homework and to prepare it better. The ability to read is at the core of much of elementary, middle, and high school achievement, and after-school programs have been shown to have important effects on reading. A National Academy of Sciences study on preventing reading difficulties confirmed that children who receive extra time and reading instruction beyond the current school day have significant improvements in their achievement.[27] Both children already succeeding in school and at-risk children benefit from after-school programs. For example, after-school tutoring in reading by volunteers has been shown to lead to improved skills of second- and third-graders who had previously been poor achievers in reading.[28] Among at-risk youth, aspirations for completing high school also improve when they participate in after-school programs, and youths are less likely both to drop out of school and to be held back. Aspira, for example, is a nationwide after-school leadership program for Latino youth, and twice as many students in Aspira have gone on to college or technical training after high school as students who have not participated.[29]

The need for quality after-school programs is great for all working families. As our studies have shown, however, children with learning disabilities have an even greater need for quality after-school assistance to help them catch up to their classmates and reach their own ability levels. After-school and vacation opportunities for school-age children with learning disabilities can make a critical difference in whether they succeed academically. To make this difference, these programs need access to the same higher staff-to-child ratios and trained specialists for helping children with learning disabilities that school-day programs have, and the services children receive need to be linked to an evaluation of the children's academic and social needs, as is currently done with services provided during the school day.

This could readily be accomplished. At present, across the United States, children with learning disabilities are taken out of the classroom during the school day—typically, multiple times a week—to work with specialists. The very children who should not be missing classroom time are pulled out and often miss reading, writing, and math in class. The bad news is that the system is backwards. The good news is that it could easily be improved dramatically. Currently, learning disability specialists typically see children during school hours (8:30 to 2:30 or 9:00 to 3:00). All they would need to do is shift their hours. If they spent the same amount of daytime hours seeing students but, instead, saw students from 11:00 to 5:00 or 12:00 to 6:00, they could work with many children with learning disabilities during after-school hours. These children would no longer be missing the classroom time they need with their grademates and would be receiving the needed extra help after school. This solution, which could make a marked difference for children, would not cost school districts additional specialists' salaries.

After-school programs, when well designed and implemented, can decrease behavioral problems as well as academic ones. Unsupervised middle school students are more than twice as likely to use drugs and alcohol.[30] When communities have more structured activities, they have fewer students suffering from major problems—including substance abuse and other behavioral and mental health problems.[31] After-school programs have also been shown to lead to a decrease in crime. This makes sense, given that the hours with the highest rates of juvenile crime occur on weekdays after school lets out, when youths are often left unsupervised. Nationwide, half of all violent juvenile crime occurs between 2:00 P.M. and 8:00 P.M.[32] After the Baltimore police started an after-school program in a high-crime area in 1995, the number of assaults and robberies fell, juvenile arrests dropped, and children's risk of being victims of a crime fell 44 percent.[33] In schools with after-school programs, school vandalism has declined; and when after-school skills-development programs have been introduced into public housing projects, juvenile arrests have dropped markedly in communities both in the United States and in Canada.[34]

In spite of all the evidence regarding their effectiveness, as noted in Chapter 3, few states have invested adequately in after-school programs. With the exception of Hawaii, in no state do more than half of all public schools have extended days. In more than half of the states, no more than one in five public schools offer after-school programs. And as noted earlier, parental demand markedly outstrips spaces nationwide. The federal government's efforts are currently focused on Twenty-First Century Community Learning Centers. This federal initiative provides limited funding to communities so that they can keep schools open longer hours and provide services for children and families during after-school hours, including, among others, tutoring, mentoring, homework centers, academic enrichment activities, sports, and arts. The idea is very promising. The centers have benefited from the collaborative support of foundations, nonprofit organizations, and businesses in their local communities. That is the good news. The problem is that they touch a fraction of the need. Federal funding of $200 million in 1999 was increased to $450 million in 2000.[35] For the more than fifty-five million school-age children in the United States, the funds amount to less than nine dollars per child per year—enough to pay for one afternoon.[36] We need to make access to quality academic extended-day and extended-year programs universal. When after-school programs are provided, we need to ensure they are high quality. The ability, training, and number of staff are all critical factors in the quality of programs. The relationship the programs have with the children's schools, families, and community are equally crucial.

Recognizing Needs and Abilities of All Ages

Every time a policy is debated that affects working families in America, we should be picturing not just a mother and an infant or toddler but fathers and mothers, teenagers and preschoolers, and grandparents who are able—if their workplaces allow them the time—to help care for their grandchildren as well as older Americans who themselves need assistance. The evidence from our national Daily Diaries Study, presented in Chapter 2, makes it clear that working Americans are daily caring for a wide range of family members. Yet the policy discussions—in both the public and the private sectors—have focused principally on parental leave for newborns and on infant and toddler care. When we consider child care for preschoolers, we need to consider child care for school-age children, as discussed above, and elder care. When we consider family leave policy, we need to recognize the wide range of caretaking relationships that working Americans have.

Until now, on family leave, as on day care, the dialogue has been restricted to a few family relationships. The FMLA allows employees to take time off to care for their parents, but not for their parents-in-law, brothers or sisters, aunts and uncles, or nieces and nephews—even if no one else is available in an emergency or even if the family member is close to death. It is hard to imagine that we want the government defining who is a close family member. Nor does it make sense for arbitrary governmental policies to determine that some Americans get care while others do not. Employers should not care about whom the leave is taken for. It makes no difference to a business whether an employee takes three days of leave to care for a child, a parent, a grandchild, or a brother. But employers clearly do have an interest in how many days of leave are taken. The amount of leave can be limited—without employers or government deciding who is family—by either or both of two methods: First, the maximum number of leave days can be set after public debate; or second, employees can be allowed leave to help a limited number of people, whom the employees select.

We need to ensure that there are affordable solutions to the daily, as well as the sporadic needs, of the elderly. The critical question of long-term care insurance—how to pay for the care of those who need twenty-four-hour nursing-home or other care—is already being debated nationally. Similar attention needs to be given to the many older women and men who can continue to live independently if they receive one to four hours of care during the day in their own homes and neighborhoods but who are unable to meet their own basic needs without that assistance. When we fail to find ways to ensure that disabled elderly individuals get small amounts of essential support in their community, too often they end up unnecessarily institutionalized at a far greater personal and economic cost.

Role of Transportation

When men and women worked out of their homes or on their farms or homesteads, the labor they conducted to produce basic goods essential for survival and their caregiving work were in the same location. One of the major changes that has occurred with the entry of men and women into the industrial and postindustrial labor force has been the physical separation of paid labor from those for whom employed adults are caring. The need for transportation and the problems surrounding that need are a natural consequence of these changes. While there has recently been some return to paid labor based in the home as a way to accommodate working families, only a minority of employed caregivers are able to work from home.[37] While the transportation dilemmas are a direct consequence of the changes in labor structure, the failure of society to make any changes in response has unnecessarily exacerbated them.

As a result of the inadequacy of public sources of transportation for children, the elderly, or ill or injured adults, one of the most frequent causes of work disruption reported in our national research was to provide transportation to family members. Lack of transportation was also one of the frequent reasons why families could not make use of available services. For example, while schools provide buses for children to attend during the short school day, even those public schools that offer before- and after-school programs commonly fail to provide any transportation for children to and from these programs. Similarly, the elderly may have health insurance so they can see a physician but no way to get to their appointments when they cannot drive or walk.

When services of any kind—health, educational, child-care, elder-care—are designed, we need to think about how children and adults will get to and from those services, given that the majority will come from families in which all working-age adults will be employed outside the home. For some services, this will mean considering distance and location issues in selecting providers. For other services, we will need to provide public transportation. If we can provide transportation for children to get to and from school, then we can provide transportation for children to get to and from before- and after-school programs. We can no longer ignore transportation issues in the provision of any services for children, the elderly, or disabled adults.

Affordable and Necessary

Can we afford to make the changes needed by American families? There's no doubt that we can afford to make the changes as a nation and that companies will survive. A quick look at surveys of the best companies for working parents shows that they currently cut across sectors, company sizes, and industries. Some are the financial leaders in their field, while others are not. There's no evidence that being among the companies to provide the best benefits has led to systematic harm. Leading companies cited by *Working Mother* magazine include large companies such as American Express, Amoco Corporation, AT&T, Bausch & Lomb, Chase Manhattan Bank, Bristol-Myers Squibb, Chrysler Corporation, Citicorp/Citibank, DuPont, and many others. Also included are smaller companies like Life Technologies, Mentor Graphics, and Neuville Industries.[38] Clearly, companies have been able to thrive while providing critically important work-family benefits. The fact remains, though, that the majority of Americans still do not have these benefits, and our own and other nations' experiences have shown that in the absence of public initiatives these problems are unlikely to be solved by the private sector alone.

What will making the needed changes on a national level mean to employers? On balance, the changes will make it easier for employers to get their essential work done well. Unnecessary absenteeism will decrease. Employees who currently must miss work because they cannot find preschool or school-age child care will not need to do so when we have the option of quality early education and extended school days available nationwide. Employees who have had to miss work to register a child for school or their family for food stamps will not need to when public services either increase their hours or expand their registration and reenrollment methods to include mail, phone, fax, or Internet. Employees who now must take off an hour and a half every day to transport a child to an after-school program will no longer need to leave work when adequate transportation services are implemented. While in some cases necessary absences will increase—such as when parents use their newly available leave time to be with sick children they might otherwise have left at home alone—these will be balanced by the drop in unnecessary absences. Whereas now, companies who offer good conditions for working families have to compete with companies who offer none, universal benefits will level the playing field nationally.

Other nations have demonstrated that economies can thrive while basic family benefits are universally provided. Paid parental leave is provided—as it has been for more than a decade—in Austria, Belgium, Canada, Denmark, Finland, France, Germany, Greece, Ireland, Italy, Netherlands, Norway, Portugal, Spain, Sweden, Switzerland, and the United Kingdom.[39] Belgium, Denmark, and Finland all guarantee child-care coverage for infants to 2-year-olds. Sweden guarantees a long parental leave period and then offers child care for those children 18 months old and older; France, for those 2 years old and older. As a result, while only 14 percent of American 3-year-olds are in publicly funded child care, 95 percent are in Belgium, as are 85 percent in Denmark, 95 percent in France, 78 percent in Germany, 88 percent in Italy, and 79 percent in Sweden.

We are far from the top in spending on elementary or secondary education. The public spending on education, as a percentage of GDP per capita, in Austria, Germany, Finland, Switzerland, Italy, and Belgium outstrips the combined public and private spending on secondary education in the United States. Likewise, the Swedes, Danes, French, Australians, and Hungarians all spend more on their combined public and private secondary education than do Americans.[40] What's more, the school year is 220 days in the Netherlands, Luxembourg, and Italy; in Germany, 213 days.[41]

Addressing the needs of working families will no more threaten our economy than providing public education or ensuring basic safety standards for workers has. In fact, like providing public education, many of the most necessary steps will strengthen our economy by providing for early and extended education for our nation's children. In the long run, our international competitiveness is determined by the quality of our labor force. Both by making it possible for all Americans

—irrespective of their income, gender, or caretaking responsibilities—to contribute in the workplace to their full potential and by improving the educational opportunities and support available to children who will join the labor force in a generation, addressing the needs of working families will strengthen our competitiveness.

We can afford the needed changes; what we cannot afford is to continue our current practices. Making changes on a national scale is necessary if all American working families are to have a chance. Perhaps most overlooked in the entire debate about addressing the needs of working families is how fundamental this effort is to equal opportunity in our country. Without it as a keystone, we will not be able to span the chasm between men's and women's daily lives and opportunities. And the gap between the opportunities that poor, middle-class, and rich children have will only grow wider.

As a nation we face critical choices. Will the inequalities women experience in the workforce continue? Will poor working parents and their children continue to face far worse odds than other families? What will happen to a sizable fraction of the middle class—particularly those families in which a child or adult has special needs? Will they all be left behind? Or will we bring our social institutions into the twenty-first century?

Much of what we need to do is not so new as to be difficult. We have provided public education for 5- to 18-year-olds; now, we need to provide it for 2- to 4-year-olds. We have school days and calendars that matched the agrarian work cycle; we need to update them to match parents' industrial and postindustrial work schedule and children's increasing need for skills. We have social security that pays attention to the income needs for older Americans; we need to pay attention to their care needs. We have national unemployment insurance that dates from when the loss of work of the single wage earner was the largest threat; we need paid family leave insurance for the current workforce when loss of work is as likely to result from the need of an adult to be home to provide care for a family member. We have adequate transportation systems for healthy adults; we need equally good ones to link children and adults in need with their caregivers. We have moved from a twelve-hour paid workday to an eight-hour one; we can move from a five-day work week to a four-and-a-half-day one. Ultimately, all that is required is the depth of commitment born of the recognition that our nation's future and our own depend on effective action.

Notes

CHAPTER 1

1. All names have been changed to protect respondents' confidentiality.
2. M. Creedon, *Issues for an Aging America: Employees and Elder Care* (Bridgeport, CT: University of Bridgeport Center for the Study of Aging, 1988). Opinion Research Corporation, *A National Survey of Caregivers: Final Report* (Washington, DC: American Association of Retired Persons and The Travelers Foundation, 1988). M. Rachor, "When Worlds Collide: Elder Caregiving Poses New Challenges for Balancing Work and Life," *The Employee Benefits Journal* 23 (3): 20–23 (1998).
3. D. Hernandez and D. Myers, *America's Children: Resources from Family, Government, and the Economy* (New York: Russell Sage Foundation, 1993).
4. D. Hernandez, "Children's Changing Access to Resources: A Historical Perspective," in *Families in the U.S.: Kinship and Domestic Politics,* ed. K. Hansen and A. Garey (Philadelphia: Temple University Press, 1998), 201–215.
5. Hernandez and Myers, *America's Children.*
6. Hernandez, "Children's Changing Access to Resources: A Historical Perspective."
7. A. Kessler-Harris, *Out to Work: A History of Wage-Earning Women in the United States* (New York: Oxford University Press, 1982).

8. C. Goldin, *Understanding the Gender Gap: An Economic History of American Women* (New York: Oxford University Press, 1990).

9. Before the war, for example, three out of five school districts refused to hire married women; after the war, only one out of five refused. Before the war, 50 percent of school districts fired women who married while employed; after the war, only 10 percent did (ibid.). When the marriage bars eroded, the rise in wage labor by married women commenced in earnest.

10. Hernandez and Myers, *America's Children*. U.S. Bureau of the Census, *Statistical Abstract of the United States: 1998* (Washington, DC, 1998).

11. Workmen's compensation, the first of these to be enacted on a wide scale, had been adopted by ten states as of 1911 and by forty-two states as of 1920; all fifty states now have such laws. At a state level, California passed the first mandatory old-age assistance in 1929, and Wisconsin adopted the first compulsory unemployment insurance in 1932; see P. Day, *A New History of Social Welfare* (Boston: Allyn and Bacon, 1997). The Social Security Act of 1935 turned income support for the elderly and unemployment insurance into federal policies and programs.

12. Congressional Research Service, *New Welfare Law: The Personal Responsibility and Work Opportunity Reconciliation Act of 1996* (96–687EPW) (Washington, DC: Library of Congress, 1996). Public L. No. 104–193, 104th Cong., 2nd sess. (August 22, 1996), *The Personal Responsibility and Work Opportunity Reconciliation Act of 1996.*

13. N. P. Gordon, P. D. Cleary, C. E. Parker, and C. A. Czeisler, "The Prevalence and Health Impact of Shiftwork," *American Journal of Public Health* 76 (10): 1225–1228 (1986). S. J. Smith, "The Growing Diversity of Work Schedules," *Monthly Labor Review* 109 (11): 7–13 (1986). H. Presser and A. Cox, "The Work Schedules of Low-Educated American Women and Welfare Reform," *Monthly Labor Review* 120 (4): 25–34 (1997). G. Silvestri, "Occupational Employment: Wide Variations in Growth," *Monthly Labor Review* 116 (11): 58–86 (1993). Increases in working hours are addressed in J. Schor, *The Overworked American: The Unexpected Decline of Leisure* (New York: Basic Books, 1992).

14. Although "work" has had the broader meaning of "activity involving mental or physical effort done in order to achieve a purpose or result," the *New Oxford Dictionary of English* (1998) defines "working" as "having paid employment" and "to employ" as "[to] give work to (someone) and pay them for it." Throughout this book the terms "employed" and "working" will be used to refer to paid employment, with the clear recognition that the unpaid work of caregiving is equally crucial and difficult. The importance of this unpaid work is, in fact, the reason for this book. The use of these terms to refer to paid and unpaid work results from the few avail-

able choices in English. Unfortunately, there is no better short way to distinguish paid and unpaid work.

15. B. Holcomb, *Not Guilty! The Good News About Working Mothers* (New York: Scribner, 1998).

16. For 1870 data, see U.S. Bureau of the Census, *Historical Statistics of the United States: Colonial Times to 1970* (Washington, DC, 1976); for 1999 data, see U.S. Bureau of the Census, "Resident Population Estimates of the United States by Age and Sex: April 1, 1990, to July 1, 1999, with Short-Term Projection to May 1, 2000," 1999. Available: http://www.census.gov/population/estimates/nation/intfile2–1.txt [2000, July 7].

CHAPTER 2

1. National Center for Health Statistics, "Number of Acute Conditions, by Age and Type of Condition: United States, 1995." Available: http://www.cdc.gov/nchs/fastats/pdf/10–199t6.pdf [2000, August 15].

2. U.S. Bureau of the Census, "Disability Status of Persons Fifteen Years Old and Over: 1994–95," in *Statistical Abstract of the United States: 1998* (Washington, DC, 1998).

3. S. Heymann, A. Earle, and B. Egleston, "Parental Availability for the Care of Sick Children," *Pediatrics* 98 (2): 226–230 (1996).

CHAPTER 3

1. U.S. Bureau of the Census, *Historical Statistics of the U.S.: Colonial Times to 1970* (Washington, DC, 1976).

2. U.S. Bureau of Labor Statistics, "Labor Force Statistics from the Current Population Survey: Annual Average Tables from the January 2000 Issue of Employment and Earnings." Available: http://stats.bls.gov/pdf/cpsaatll.pdf [2000, June 26].

3. U.S. Department of Education, "Safe and Smart: Making After-School Hours Work for Kids—June 1998." Available: http://www.ed.gov/pubs/SafeandSmart/intro.html [2000, July 13].

4. General Accounting Office, *Welfare Reform: Implications of Increased Work Participation for Child Care* (Washington, DC, 1997).

5. Children's Defense Fund, *Child Care Challenges* (Washington, DC: Children's Defense Fund, 1998).

6. E. F. Mellor, "Shift Work and Flexitime: How Prevalent Are They?" *Monthly Labor Review* 109 (11): 14–21 (1986).

7. N. P. Gordon, P. D. Cleary, C. E. Parker, and C. A. Czeisler, "The Prevalence and Health Impact of Shiftwork," *American Journal of Public Health* 76 (10): 1225–1228 (1986). S. J. Smith, "The Growing Diversity of Work

Schedules," *Monthly Labor Review* 109 (11): 7–13 (1986). U.S. Bureau of the Census, *Statistical Abstract of the United States: 1993* (Washington, DC, 1993).

8. P. Seppanen, A. Love, D. Kaplan-DeVries, L. Bernstein, M. Seligson, F. Marx, and E. Kisker, *National Study of Before- and After-School Programs: A Report to the Office of Policy and Planning, U.S. Department of Education* (Portsmouth, NH: RMC Research Corporation, 1993).

9. U.S. Department of Labor Women's Bureau, "Care Around the Clock: Developing Childcare Resources Before 9 and After 5," 1995. Available: http://www.dol.gov/dol/wb/public/media/reports/care.htm//execsum [2000, September 1].

10. H. Presser and A. Cox, "The Work Schedules of Low-Educated American Women and Welfare Reform," *Monthly Labor Review* 120 (4): 25–34 (1997).

11. Congressional Research Service, *New Welfare Law: The Personal Responsibility and Work Opportunity Reconciliation Act of 1996* (96–687EPW) (Washington, DC: Library of Congress, 1996).

12. Presser and Cox, "The Work Schedules of Low-Educated American Women."

13. G. Silvestri, "Occupational Employment: Wide Variations in Growth," *Monthly Labor Review* 116 (11): 58–86 (1993).

14. J. C. Gornick, M. K. Meyers, and K. E. Ross, "Supporting the Employment of Mothers: Policy Variation Across Fourteen Welfare States," *Journal of European Social Policy* 7 (1): 45–69 (1997).

15. Children's Defense Fund, "Children in the States: 1998 Data." Available: http://www.childrensdefense.org/states/data.html [1998, April 28].

16. President William Jefferson Clinton, State of the Union Address, 1999. White House Office of the Press Secretary. Available: http://www.pub.whitehouse.gov/uri-res/I2R?urn:pdi://oma.eop.gov.us/1999/1/20/1.text.1 [1999, August 16].

17. Children's Defense Fund, "Child Care Challenges." Available: http://www.childrensdefensefund.org/childcare/challenges/cc–challenges.html [2000, July 14].

18. National Center for Education Statistics, "Table 161. Revenues for Public Elementary and Secondary Schools, by Source and State: 1996–7." Available: http://nces.ed.gov/pubs2000/digest99/d99t161.html [2000, July 11].

19. B. Iverson, G. Brownlee, and H. Walberg, "Parent-Teacher Contacts and Student Learning," *Journal of Educational Research* 74 (6): 394–396 (1981). D. Stevenson and D. Baker, "The Family-School Relation and the Child's School Performance," *Child Development* 58 (5): 1348–1357 (1987). R. Bradley, S. Rock, B. Caldwell, P. Harris, and H. Hamrick, "Home Environment and School Performance Among Black Elementary School Children," *Journal of Negro Education* 56 (4): 499–509 (1987).

20. T. Keith, P. Keith, G. Troutman, P. Bickley, P. Trivette, and K. Singh, "Does

Parental Involvement Affect Eighth-Grade Student Achievement? Structural Analysis of National Data," *School Psychology Review* 22 (3): 474–496 (1993). P. Fehrmann, T. Keith, and T. Reimers, "Home Influence on School Learning: Direct and Indirect Effects of Parental Involvement on High School Grades," *Journal of Educational Research* 80 (6): 330–337 (1987).

21. A. Reynolds, "Comparing Measures of Parental Involvement and Their Effects on Academic Achievement," *Early Childhood Research Quarterly* 7 (3): 441–462 (1992). J. Griffith, "Relation of Parental Involvement, Empowerment, and School Traits to Student Academic Performance," *Journal of Educational Research* 90 (1): 33–41 (1996). S. Christenson, T. Rounds, and D. Gorney, "Family Factors and Student Achievement: An Avenue to Increase Students' Success," *School Psychology Quarterly* 7 (3): 178–206 (1992). D. Miller and M. Kelley, "Interventions for Improving Homework Performance: A Critical Review," *School Psychology Quarterly* 6 (3): 174–185 (1991). J. Comer, "Home-School Relationships as They Affect the Academic Success of Children," *Education and Urban Society* 16 (3): 323–337 (1984). J. Fantuzzo, G. Davis, and M. Ginsburg, "Effects of Parent Involvement in Isolation or in Combination with Peer Tutoring on Student Self-Concept and Mathematics Achievement," *Journal of Educational Psychology* 87 (2): 272–281 (1995).

22. I. Kristensson-Hallstron, G. Elander, and G. Malmfors, "Increased Parental Participation on a Pediatric Surgical Daycare Unit," *Journal of Clinical Nursing* 6: 297–302 (1997). S. J. Palmer, "Care of Sick Children by Parents: A Meaningful Role," *Journal of Advanced Nursing* 18 (2): 185–191 (1993). G. van der Schyff, "The Role of Parents During Their Child's Hospitalisation," *Australian Nurses Journal* 8 (11): 57–58, 61 (1979). J. Robertson, *Young Children in Hospitals* (New York: Basic Books, 1958). P. R. Mahaffy, "The Effects of Hospitalization on Children Admitted for Tonsillectomy and Adenoidectomy," *Nursing Research* 14 (1): 12–19 (1965). J. Bowlby, *Child Care and the Growth of Love* (Baltimore: Penguin Books, 1953).

23. M. Taylor and P. O'Connor, "Resident Parents and Shorter Hospital Stay," *Archives of Disease in Childhood* 64 (2): 274–276 (1989).

24. A. George and J. Hancock, "Reducing Pediatric Burn Pain with Parent Participation," *Journal of Burn Care and Rehabilitation* 14 (1): 104–107 (1993). P. LaRosa Nash and J. Murphy, "An Approach to Pediatric Perioperative Care: Parent—Present Induction," *Nursing Clinics of North America* 32 (1): 183–199 (1997).

25. S. Heymann, S. Toomey, and F. Furstenberg. "Working Parents: What Factors Are Involved in Their Ability to Take Time Off from Work When Their Children Are Sick?" *Archives of Pediatrics and Adolescent Medicine* 153 (8): 870–874 (1999).

26. M. Mottonen and M. Uhari, "Absences for Sickness Among Children in Day Care," *Acta Paediatrica* (81) 11: 929–932 (1992). R. Haskins, "Day Care and Illness: Evidence, Costs, and Public Policy," *Pediatrics* 77 (6), part 2, suppl.: 951–982 (1986). P. Sullivan, W. E. Woodward, L. K. Pickering, and H. L. Dupont, "Longitudinal Study of Occurrence of Diarrheal Disease in Day Care Centers," *American Journal of Public Health* 74 (9): 987–991 (1984). A. B. Doyle, "Incidence of Illness in Early Group and Family Day-Care," *Pediatrics* 58 (4): 607–613 (1976). K. Strangert, "Respiratory Illness in Preschool Children with Different Forms of Day Care," *Pediatrics* 57 (2): 191–196 (1976). F. A. Loda, W. P. Glezen, and W. A. Clyde Jr., "Respiratory Disease in Group Day Care," *Pediatrics* 49 (3): 428–437 (1972).

For data on other nations, see S. D. Hillis, C. M. Miranda, M. McCann, D. Bender, and K. Weigle, "Day Care Center Attendance and Diarrheal Morbidity in Colombia," *Pediatrics* 90 (4): 582–588 (1992); M. A. Oyediran and A. Bamisaiye, "A Study of the Child-Care Arrangements and the Health Status of Pre-School Children of Employed Women in Lagos," *Public Health* (London) 97 (5): 267–274 (1983); and I. L. Dahl, M. Grufman, C. Hellberg, and M. Krabbe, "Absenteeism Because of Illness at Daycare Centers and in Three-Family Systems," *Acta Paediatrica Scandinavica* 80 (4): 436–445 (1991).

For early studies conducted, see I. Diehl, "The Prevalence of Colds in Nursery School Children and Non–Nursery School Children," *Journal of Pediatrics* 34: 52–61 (1949); E. Frisell, "A Comparison Between the Sedimentation Rates of Children in Day-Nurseries and Children Cared For in Their Homes," *Acta Paediatrica* 35: 1–9 (1948); and L. Hesselvik, "Respiratory Infections Among Children in Day Nurseries," *Acta Paediatrica* 74 (suppl.): 96–103 (1949).

27. J. Schor, *The Overworked American: The Unexpected Decline of Leisure* (New York: Basic Books, 1992).

CHAPTER 4

1. A. Hochschild, *The Second Shift* (New York: Avon Books, 1989).
2. U.S. Bureau of the Census, "Disability Status of Persons Less Than Twenty-Two Years Old: 1994–95." Available: http://www.census.gov/hhes/www/disable/sipp/disab9495/ds94t2.html [2000, July 6].
3. L. Aron, P. Loprest, and C. Steuerle, Serving *Children with Disabilities: A Systematic Look at the Programs* (Washington, DC: The Urban Institute Press, 1996). K. Johnson, "Children with Special Health Needs: Ensuring Appropriate Coverage and Care Under Health Care Reform," *Health Policy and Child Health* 1 (3): 1–5 (1994). P. Newacheck, B. Strickland, J.

Shonkoff, et al., "An Epidemiologic Profile of Children with Special
Health Care Needs," *Pediatrics* 102 (1): 117–123 (1998).
4. C. Wolman, M. Resnick, L. Harris, and R. Blum, "Emotional Well-Being
Among Adolescents With and Without Chronic Conditions," *Journal of
Adolescent Health* 15 (3): 199–204 (1994). K. Hamlett, D. Pellegrini, and
K. Katz, "Childhood Chronic Illness as a Family Stressor," *Journal of
Pediatric Psychology* 17 (1): 33–47 (1992).
For epilepsy, see S. Carlton-Ford, R. Miller, M. Brown, N. Nealeigh, and P.
Jennings, "Epilepsy and Children's Social and Psychological Adjustment,"
Journal of Health and Social Behavior 36 (3): 285–301 (1995).
For diabetes, see B. Anderson, J. Miller, W. Auslander, and J. Santiago, "Family
Characteristics of Diabetic Adolescents: Relationship to Metabolic
Control," *Diabetes Care* 4 (6): 586–594 (1981); C. Hanson, M. De Guire,
A. Schinkel, S. Henggeler, and G. Burghen, "Comparing Social Learning
and Family Systems Correlates of Adaptation in Youths with IDDM,"
Journal of Pediatric Psychology 17 (5): 555–572 (1992); and A. La Greca,
W. Auslander, P. Greco, D. Spetter, E. J. Fisher, and J. Santiago, "I Get By
with a Little Help from My Family and Friends: Adolescents' Support for
Diabetes Care," *Journal of Pediatric Psychology* 20 (4): 449–476 (1995).
5. Anderson, Miller, Auslander, and Santiago, "Family Characteristics of
Diabetic Adolescents." Hanson, De Guire, Schinkel, Henggeler, and
Burghen, "Comparing Social Learning and Family Systems Correlates."
C. Hanson, M. De Guire, A. Schinkel, and O. Kolterman, "Empirical
Validation for a Family-Centered Model of Care," *Diabetes Care* 18 (10):
1347–1356 (1995).
6. La Greca, Auslander, Greco, Spetter, Fisher, and Santiago, "I Get By with a
Little Help from My Family and Friends."
7. S. Hauser, A. Jacobson, P. Lavori, et al., "Adherence Among Children and
Adolescents with Insulin-Dependent Diabetes Mellitus over a Four-Year
Longitudinal Follow-Up: II. Immediate and Long-Term Linkages with
the Family Milieu," *Journal of Pediatric Psychology* 15 (4): 527–542
(1990). E. Holden, D. Chmielewski, C. Nelson, V. Kager, and L. Foltz,
"Controlling for General and Disease-Specific Effects in Child and
Family Adjustment to Chronic Childhood Illness," *Journal of Pediatric
Psychology* 22 (1): 15–27 (1997). S. Johnson, "Family Management of
Childhood Diabetes," *Journal of Clinical Psychology in Medical Settings* 1
(4): 309–315 (1994).
8. Hamlett, Pellegrini, and Katz, "Childhood Chronic Illness as a Family
Stressor." Wolman, Resnick, Harris, and Blum, "Emotional Well-Being
Among Adolescents With and Without Chronic Conditions."
9. These analyses were conducted using the National Longitudinal Survey of
Youth described in Appendix B.
10. U.S. Department of Health and Human Services, "Disabilities Among Children

Aged Less Than or Equal to Seventeen Years: United States, 1991–1992," *Morbidity and Mortality Weekly Report* 44 (33): 609–613 (1995).

11. E. M. Lewit and L. S. Baker, "Children in Special Education," *The Future of Children* 6 (1): 139–151 (1996).

12. M. D. Clark, "Teacher Response to Learning Disability: A Test of Attributional Principles," *Journal of Learning Disabilities* 30 (1): 69–79 (1997).

13. V. Pearson and T. W. L. Chan, "The Relationship Between Parenting Stress and Social Support in Mothers of Children with Learning Disabilities: A Chinese Experience," *Social Science and Medicine* 37 (2): 267–274 (1993).

14. C. Geisthardt and J. Munsch, "Coping with School Stress: A Comparison of Adolescents With and Without Learning Disabilities," *Journal of Learning Disabilities* 29 (3): 287–296 (1996).

15. M. M. Wagner and J. Blackorby, "Transitions from High School to Work or College: How Special Education Students Fare," *The Future of Children* 6 (1): 103–120 (1996).

16. K. Jost, "Learning Disabilities," *CQ Researcher* 3 (46): 1081–1104 (1993).

17. Wagner and Blackorby, "Transitions from High School to Work or College."

18. A. G. Ryan, "Life Adjustments of College Freshmen With and Without Learning Disabilities," *Annals of Dyslexia* 44: 227–249 (1994).

19. Wagner and Blackorby, "Transitions from High School to Work or College." P. L. Sitlington, A. R. Frank, and R. Carson, "Adult Adjustment Among High School Graduates with Mild Disabilities," *Exceptional Children* 59 (3): 221–233 (1993).

20. Wagner and Blackorby, "Transitions from High School to Work or College." M. J. Karpinski, D. A. Neubert, and S. Graham, "A Follow-Along Study of Postsecondary Outcomes for Graduates and Dropouts with Mild Disabilities in a Rural Setting," *Journal of Learning Disabilities* 25 (6): 376–385 (1992).

21. D. Yasutake, T. Bryan, and E. Dohrn, "The Effects of Combining Peer Tutoring and Attribution Training on Students' Perceived Self-Competence" *Remedial and Special Education* 17 (2): 83–91 (1996).

22. H. R. Rothman and M. Cosden, "The Relationship Between Self-Perception of a Learning Disability and Achievement, Self-Concept, and Social Support," *Learning Disability Quarterly* 18 (3): 203–212 (1995). H. L. Swanson and S. Malone, "Social Skills and Learning Disabilities: A Meta-Analysis of the Literature," *School Psychology Review* 21 (3): 427–443 (1992). H. E. Rawson and J. C. Cassady, "Effects of Therapeutic Intervention on Self-Concepts of Children with Learning Disabilities," *Child and Adolescent Social Work Journal* 12 (1): 19–31 (1995).

23. Geisthardt and Munsch, "Coping with School Stress."

24. E. N. Patrikakou, "Investigating the Academic Achievement of Adolescents with Learning Disabilities: A Structural Modeling Approach," *Journal of Educational Psychology* 88 (3): 435–450 (1996).

25. G. R. Lyon, "Learning Disabilities," *The Future of Children* 6 (1): 54–76 (1996).
26. K. P. Barnett, H. F. Clarizio, and K. A. Payette, "Grade Retention Among Students with Learning Disabilities," *Psychology in the Schools* 33 (4): 285–293 (1996).
27. R. S. Byrd and M. L. Weitzman, "Predictors of Early Grade Retention Among Children in the United States," *Pediatrics* 93 (3): 481–487 (1994).
28. U.S. Code of Federal Regulations, Title 34, Individuals with Disabilities Education Act, Section 300 (1991), and U.S. Code of Federal Regulations, Title 45, Head Start Act, Section 1301 (1965). Support services can include lower student-teacher ratios in special-education classrooms, additional staffing for regular classrooms, sessions with specialists, and special training for classroom teachers, among other things.
29. L. Montgomery, J. Kiely, and G. Pappas, "The Effects of Poverty, Race, and Family Structure on U.S. Children's Health: Data from the NHIS, 1978 through 1980 and 1989 through 1991," *American Journal of Public Health* 86 (10): 1401–1405 (1996). B. Starfield, "Effects of Poverty on Health Status," *Bulletin of the New York Academy of Medicine* 68 (1): 17–24 (1992). R. Issler, E. Giugliani, G. Kreutz, et al., "Poverty Levels and Children's Health Status: Study of Risk Factors in an Urban Population of Low Socioeconomic Level," *Revista de Saude Publica* 30 (6): 506–511 (1996). V. McLoyd, "The Impact of Economic Hardship on Black Families and Children: Psychological Distress, Parenting, and Socioemotional Development," *Child Development* 61 (2): 311–346 (1990). R. Anker, *Gender and Jobs: Sex Segregation of Occupations in the World* (Geneva: International Labor Office, 1998). R. Bradley, L. Whiteside, D. Mundfrom, P. Casey, K. Kelleher, and S. Pope, "Early Indications of Resilience and Their Relation to Experiences in the Home Environments of Low Birthweight, Premature Children Living in Poverty," *Child Development* 65(2): 346–360 (1994). P. McGauhey, B. Starfield, C. Alexander, and M. Ensminger, "Social Environment and Vulnerability of Low Birth Weight Children: A Social-Epidemiological Perspective," *Pediatrics* 88(5): 943–953 (1991). J. Watson, R. Kirby, K. Kelleher, and R. Bradley, "Effects of Poverty on Home Environment: An Analysis of Three-Year Outcome Data for Low Birth Weight Premature Infants," *Journal of Pediatric Psychology* 21(3): 419–431 (1996).

CHAPTER 5

1. M. Szinovacz, "Grandparents Today: A Demographic Profile," *The Gerontologist* 38 (1): 37–52 (1998). R. Pruchno and K. Johnson, "Research on Grandparenting: Review of Current Studies and Future Needs," *Generations* 20 (1): 65–70 (1996).

2. U.S. Bureau of the Census, *Statistical Abstract of the United States: 1997* (Washington, DC, 1997).

3. J. Treas and R. Torrecilha, "The Older Population," in *State of the Union: America in the 1990s,* vol. 2, *Social Trends,* ed. R. Farley (New York: Russell Sage Foundation, 1995), 47–92.

4. U.S. Bureau of the Census, *Historical Statistics of the United States: Colonial Times to 1970* (Washington, DC, 1976).

5. U.S. Bureau of the Census, "Resident Population Estimates of the United States by Age and Sex: April 1, 1990, to July 1, 1999, with Short-Term Projection to April 1, 2000." Available: http://www.census.gov/population/estimates/nation/intfile2–1.txt [1999, November 19].

6. U.S. Bureau of the Census, "Projections of the Population by Age, Sex, Race, and Hispanic Origin for the United States: 1999 to 2100." Available: http://www.census.gov/population/projections/nation/detail/d2021–30.pdf [2000, July 14].

7. U.N. Department of Economic and Social Development, Statistical Division, *1991 Demographic Yearbook* (1992), Table 7.

8. U.S. Bureau of the Census, "Disability Status of Persons Fifteen Years Old and Over: 1994–95," in *Statistical Abstract of the United States, 1998* (Washington, DC, 1998).

9. As not only longevity but also years of healthy life increase, the meaningful age definitions of "young-old" and "old-old" will need to be extended. The age categories cited in the text are based on the work of Neugarten, Treas, and Torrecilha. See B. Neugarten, "Age Groups in American Society and the Rise of the Young-Old," *Annals of the American Academy of Political and Social Science* 415 (September): 187–198 (1974); Treas and Torrecilha, "The Older Population."

10. Treas and Torrecilha, "The Older Population."

11. Ibid.

12. U.S. Bureau of the Census, "Table 20. Voting and Registration: November 1990." Available: http://www.census.gov/population/socdemo/voting/history/vot20.txt [2000, July 17].

13. U.S. Bureau of the Census, "Table 2. Percent Reported Voting and Registering in Congressional Election Years, by Age and Region of Residence: November 1966 to 1994." Available: http://www.census.gov/population/socdemo/voting/history/htable02.txt [2000, July 12].

14. R. Burkhauser and D. Salisbury, eds., *Pensions in a Changing Economy* (Washington, DC: Employee Benefit Research Institute, Education and Research Fund, 1993).

15. U.S. Bureau of the Census, "Table 3. Poverty Status of People, by Age, Race, and Hispanic Origin: 1959 to 1998." Available:

http://www.census.gov/hhes/poverty/histpov/hstpov3.html [2000, February 9].

16. Treas and Torrecilha, "The Older Population."

17. L. Achdut and Y. Tamir, "Retirement and Well-Being Among the Elderly in Poverty: Inequality in Income Distribution in Comparative Perspective," in *Poverty, Inequality, and Income Distribution in Comparative Perspective: The Luxembourg Income Study*, ed. T. Smeeding, M. O'Higgins, and L. Rainwater (New York: Harvester Wheatsheaf, 1990), 105–125.

18. E. Kassner and L. Williams, *Taking Care of Their Own: State-Funded Home and Community-Based Care Programs for Older Persons* (Washington, DC: AARP Public Policy Institute, 1997). J. O'Keeffe, *Determining the Need for Long-Term Care Services: An Analysis of Health and Functional Eligibility Criteria in Medicaid Home and Community-Based Waiver Programs* (Washington, DC: AARP Public Policy Institute, 1996).

CHAPTER 6

1. S. Heymann and A. Earle, "The Impact of Welfare Reform on Parents' Ability to Care for Their Children's Health," *American Journal of Public Health* 89 (4): 502–505 (1999).

2. A. Earle and S. Heymann, "Work, Family, and Social Class," in *A Portrait of Midlife in the U.S.*, ed. R. Kessler and C. Ryff (Chicago: University of Chicago Press, forthcoming).

3. Children's Defense Fund, "Helping Parents Work and Children Learn." Available: http://www.childrensdefense.org/childcare/cc_facts.html [2000, June 27].

4. U.S. Bureau of the Census, *Statistical Abstract of the United States: 1996* (Washington, DC, 1996).

5. U.S. Bureau of the Census, *Statistical Abstract of the United States: 1991* (Washington, DC, 1991).

6. Child Care Bureau, "Child Care for Young Children: Quality." Available: http://www.acf.dhhs.gov/programs/ccb/faq/quality.htm [1999, December 17].

7. Commission on Family and Medical Leave, *A Workable Balance: Report to Congress on Family and Medical Leave Policies* (Washington, DC: U.S. Department of Labor, 1996).

CHAPTER 7

1. W. Chafe, *The Paradox of Change: American Women in the 20th Century* (New York: Oxford University Press, 1991).

2. Chafe, *The Paradox of Change*.

3. C. Goldin, *Understanding the Gender Gap: An Economic History of American Women* (New York: Oxford University Press, 1990).

4. D. Cobble, *Women and Unions: Forging a Partnership* (Ithaca: ILR Press, Cornell University, 1993).

5. D. Balser, *Sisterhood and Solidarity: Feminism and Labor in Modern Times* (Boston: South End Press, 1987).

6. Chafe, *The Paradox of Change*. As late as the 1960s, more than one in four unions reported having no women members, and in more than half, women made up 10 percent or less of the membership. Even when the labor movement's composition began to change as an increasing number of women entered the paid labor force and as sectors of the economy with large numbers of female employees—including education, health, and government—became unionized, few women were allowed at the top of union leadership. Not until 1955 was a woman elected to the AFL-CIO executive council, and not until 1981 was the second woman elected. In the 1990s, while formal exclusion of women no longer persisted and while women were joining unions in the United States at three times the rate of men, women were still less likely to hold office. See A. Kessler-Harris, *Out to Work: A History of Wage-Earning Women in the United States* (New York: Oxford University Press, 1982); Goldin, *Understanding the Gender Gap*.

7. Male Help Wanted Ads, Female Help Wanted Ads, in the *Boston Sunday Globe*, June 16, 1940.

8. Goldin, *Understanding the Gender Gap*.

9. Male Help Wanted Ads, Female Help Wanted Ads, *Boston Daily*, Thursday, June 22, 1950.

10. Men Wanted Ads, *Boston Globe*, Friday, August 21, 1970.

11. Female Help Wanted Ads, *Boston Sunday Globe*, August 23, 1970.

12. U.S. Bureau of the Census, *The Statistical History of the United States: From Colonial Times to the Present*, vol. 303 (New York: Basic Books, 1976).

13. Goldin, *Understanding the Gender Gap*.

14. V. R. Fuchs, ed., *Women's Quest for Economic Equality* (Cambridge, MA: Harvard University Press, 1988).

15. Institute for Women's Policy Research, *The Status of Women in the States* (Washington, DC: Institute for Women's Policy Research, 1996).

16. J. Waldfogel, "Women Working for Less: Family Status and Women's Pay in the U.S. and the U.K.," working paper no. D–94–1, Malcom Wiener Center for Social Policy, Harvard University, 1994.

17. Fuchs, *Women's Quest for Economic Equality*.

18. Ibid.

19. U.S. Bureau of the Census, "Employed Civilians, by Occupation, Sex, Race, and Hispanic Origin: 1983 and 1997." Available:

http://www.census.gov/prod/3/98pubs/98statab/sasec13.pdf [2000, February 22].

20. J. Schor, *The Overworked American: The Unexpected Decline of Leisure* (New York: Basic Books, 1992).

21. Reformers for women's rights had begun working alongside antislavery reformers in the mid-1800s, initially believing the fight for equal rights for women and African-Americans should be waged simultaneously.

22. M. Anderson, *Women at Work* (Minneapolis: University of Minnesota Press, 1951). Chafe, *The Paradox of Change.*

23. J. Mansbridge, *Why We Lost the ERA* (Chicago: University of Chicago Press, 1986).W. Chafe, *The American Woman: Her Changing Social, Economic, and Political Roles, 1920–1970* (New York: Oxford University Press, 1972).

24. C. Goldin, "Career and Family: College Women Look to the Past," in *Gender and Family Issues in the Workplace,* ed. F. D. Blau and R. G. Ehrenberg (New York: Russell Sage Foundation, 1997), 20–58. J. Waldfogel, "Working Mothers Then and Now: A Cross-Cohort Analysis of the Effects of Maternity Leave on Women's Pay," in Blau and Ehrenberg, *Gender and Family Issues in the Workplace,* 92–126.

25. Catalyst, "The 1998 Catalyst Census of Women Board Directors of the Fortune 500." Available: http://www.catalystwomen.org/press/facts1998wbd.html. [1999, November 18].

26. Catalyst, "1999 Catalyst Census of Women Corporate Officers and Top Earners." Available: http://www.catalystwomen.org/press/factscote99.html. [1999, November 18].

27. Center for the American Woman and Politics, Eagleton Institute of Politics–Rutgers University, "Women in Elective Office. 2000 Fact Sheet Summaries." Available: http://rci.rutgers.edu/~cawp/facts/cawpfs.html [2000, July 17].

28. Blau and Ehrenberg, *Gender and Family Issues in the Workplace.*

29. R. Farley, ed., *State of the Union: America in the 1990s* (New York: Russell Sage Foundation, 1995).

30. J. C. Gornick, M. K. Meyers, and K. E. Ross, "Public Policies in the Employment of Mothers: A Cross National Study," *Science Quarterly* 79: 35–54 (1998).

CHAPTER 8

1. K. E. Heintz-Knowles, "Balancing Acts: Work/Family Issues on Prime-Time TV," research report commissioned by the National Partnership for Women and Families, National Partnership for Women and Families, 1998.

2. Heintz-Knowles, "Balancing Acts."
3. Children's Defense Fund, "Polls Indicate Widespread Support for Increased Investments in Child Care." Available: http://www.childrensdefense-fund.org/childcare/cc_polls.html [2000, February 29].
4. S. Hewlett and W. Cornel, *The War Against Parents: What We Can Do for America's Beleaguered Moms and Dads* (New York: Houghton Mifflin, 1998).
5. Ibid.
6. National Partnership for Women and Families, "Family Matters:A National Survey of Women and Men." Available: http://www.nationalpartnership.org/survey/survey3.htm [2000, July 12].
7. Ibid.
8. S. Coontz, *The Way We Never Were: American Families and the Nostalgia Trap* (New York: Basic Books, 1992).
9. O. S. Mitchel, "Work and Family Benefits," in *Gender and Family Issues in the Workplace,* ed. F. D. Blau and R. G. Ehrenberg (New York: Russell Sage Foundation, 1997), 269–276.
10. N. Folbre, *Who Pays for the Kids? Gender and the Structures of Constraint* (London: Routledge, 1994).
11. In this context, the amount families are investing in children and the number of Americans having children are declining. In the ten years from 1985 to 1995, there was a 10 percent decline in fertility rates (from 69 births per 1,000 reproductive-age women to 61 births per 1,000 reproductive-age women). U.S. Bureau of the Census, "Percent Childless and Births per 1,000 Women in the Last Year: Selected Years, June 1976 to Present." Available: http://www.census.gov/population/socdemo/fertility/fert95/tabH1.txt [2000, February 29].
12. U.S. Department of Labor, Bureau of Labor Statistics, "Employee Benefits in Medium and Large Private Establishments, 1997." Available: http://www.bls.gov/ebs2/ebnr0005.pdf [2000, July 17].
13. U.S. Department of Labor, Bureau of Labor Statistics, "Employee Benefits in Small Private Establishments, 1996." Available: http://www.bls.gov/ebs2/ebnr0004.pdf [2000, July 17].
14. Women, Infants, and Children (WIC) is a program providing education, nutritional supplementation, and access to health services for low-income pregnant and breast-feeding women and preschool children.
15. J. Currie and D. Thomas, "Does Head Start Make a Difference?" *American Economic Review* 85 (3): 341–364 (1995).
16. R. McKay, L. Condell, and H. Ganson, *The Impact of Head Start on Children, Families and Communities: Final Report of the Head Start Evaluation, Synthesis, and Utilization Project* (Washington, DC: CSR Inc., 1985).

17. W. Barnett, "Long-Term Effects of Early Childhood Programs on Cognitive and School Outcomes," *The Future of Children* 5 (3): 25–50 (1995). F. Campbell and C. Ramey, "Effects of Early Intervention on Intellectual and Academic Achievement: A Follow-Up Study of Children from Low-Income Families," *Child Development* 65 (2): 684–698 (1994). D. Johnson and T. Walker, "A Follow-Up Evaluation of the Houston Parent-Child Development Center: School Performance," *Journal of Early Intervention* 15 (3): 226–236 (1991). S. Andrews, J. Blumenthal, D. Johnson et al., "The Skills of Mothering: A Study of Parent Child Development Centers," *Monographs of the Society for Research in Child Development* 47(6): 1–83 (1982). H. Garber, *The Milwaukee Project: Preventing Mental Retardation in Children at Risk* (Washington, DC: American Association on Mental Retardation, 1988).

18. National Center for Education Statistics, "Table 55–4. Expenditures per Student for Early Childhood Education, 1993." Available: http://nces.ed.gov/pubs/ce/c97p55.pdf [2000, July 11].

19. Urban Institute, *Children's Budget Report: A Detailed Analysis of Spending on Low-Income Children's Programs in Thirteen States* (Washington, DC: Urban Institute, 1998).

20. K. Shulman and G. Adams, *A High Cost of Childcare Puts Quality Care Out of Reach for Many Families: Children's Defense Fund* (Washington, DC: Children's Defense Fund, 1998).

21. Data on Head Start enrollment reported by Craig Turner, Head Start Bureau, in a telephone interview by Maria Palacios on March 7, 2000, based on *Head Start Program Information Report* (September 1998–June 1999) and data from Head Start Bureau databases.

22. National Center for Education Statistics, "Table 39. Historical Summary of Public Elementary and Secondary School Statistics: 1869–70 to 1996–97." Available: http://nces.ed.gov/pubs2000/digest99/d99t039.html [2000, July 11].

23. Ibid.

24. National Center for Education Statistics, "Table 403. Average Eighth Grade Mathematics Scores, by Content Areas, and Average Time Spent Studying Mathematics Out of School, by Country: 1994–95." Available: http//nces.ed.gov/pubs2000/digest99/d99t403.html [2000, July 7].

25. National Center for Education Statistics, "Table 405. Average Eighth Grade Science Scores, by Content Areas, and Average Time Spent Studying Science Out of School, by Country: 1994–95." Available: http//nces.ed.gov/pubs2000/digest99/d99t405.html [2000, August 15].

26. J. Posner and D. Vandell, "Low-Income Children's After-School Care: Are There Beneficial Effects of After-School Programs?" *Child Development* 65 (2): 440–456 (1994). Department of Education, "Safe and Smart:

Making After-School Hours Work for Kids—June 1998." Available: http://www.ed.gov/pubs/SafeandSmart [2000, July 6].

27. C. Snow, *Preventing Reading Difficulties in Young Children* (Washington, DC: National Research Council and National Academy of Sciences, 1998).

28. D. Morris, B. Shaw, and J. Perney, "Helping Low Readers in Grades 2 and 3: An After-School Volunteer Tutoring Program," *Elementary School Journal* 91 (2): 133–150 (1990).

29. J. Funkhouser, *Extending the Learning Time for Disadvantaged Students* (Washington, DC: Department of Education, 1995).

30. J. L. Richardson, K. Dwyer, K. McGuigan, W. B. Hansen, C. Dent, C. A. Johnson, S. Y. Sussman, B. Brannon, and B. Flay, "Substance Abuse Among Eighth-Grade Students Who Take Care of Themselves After School," *Pediatrics* 84 (3): 556–566 (1989).

31. D. Blyth and N. Leffert, "Communities as Contexts for Adolescent Development: An Empirical Analysis," *Journal of Adolescent Research* 10 (1): 64–87 (1995)

32. M. Sickmund, H. Snyder, and E. Poe-Yamagata, *Juvenile Offenders and Victims: 1997 Update on Violence* (Washington, DC: U.S. Department of Justice, Office of Juvenile Justice and Delinquency Prevention, 1997).

33. Department of Education, "Safe and Smart: Making After-School Hours Work for Kids," June 1998. Available: http://www.ed.gov/pubs/SafeandSmart [2000, July 6].

34. J. Fox and S. Newman, *After-School Crime or After-School Programs: Tuning in the Prime Time for Violent Juvenile Crime and Implications for National Policy* (Washington, DC: Fight Crime Invest in Kids, 1997). P. Schinke, M. Orlandi, and K. Cole, "Boys and Girls Clubs in Public Housing Developments: Prevention Services for Youth at Risk," *Journal of Community Psychology,* OSAP special issue, 1992.

35. Twenty-First Century Community Learning Centers. Available: http://www.ed.gov/21stcclc/index.html [2000, March 1].

36. U.S. Bureau of the Census, "Resident Population Estimates of the United States by Age and Sex: April 1, 1990, to July 1, 1999, with Short-Term Projection to April 1, 2000." Available: http://www.census.gov/population/estimates/nation/intfile2–1.txt [2000, March 8].

37. Current Population Survey, "Work at Home in 1997." Available: http://bls.gov/news.release/homey.nws.htm [2000, September 1].

38. "The Hundred Best Companies for Working Mothers," *Working Mother,* October 1998.

39. C. J. Rhum and J. L. Teague, "Parental Leave Policies in Europe and North America," working paper no. 5065, National Bureau of Economic Research, Cambridge, MA, 1995.

40. National Center for Education Statistics, "Table 55–6. Expenditures per

Student for Secondary Education: 1993." Available: http://nces.ed.gov/pubs/ce/c97p55.pdf [2000, July 11].

41. J. C. Gornick, M. K. Meyers, and K. E. Ross, "Supporting the Employment of Mothers: Policy Variation Across Fourteen Welfare States," *Journal of European Social Policy* 7 (1): 45–69 (1997)

Appendix A

Twentieth-Century Demographic
Shifts in Labor

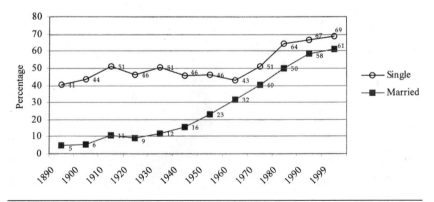

FIGURE A.1   Labor Force Participation Rate of Single and Married Women, 1890–1999

NOTE: The figure is based on data for 1890 to 1970 from U.S. Bureau of the Census, *Historical Statistics of the United States: Colonial Times to 1970,* part 1, series D 49–62, 1890–1970, decennial census (Washington, DC, 1976), 133; for 1980 to 1990, U.S. Bureau of the Census, *Statistical Abstract of the United States: 1997* (Washington, DC, 1997); for 1999 from U.S. Bureau of Labor Statistics, unpublished tabulations calculated from the Current Population Survey.

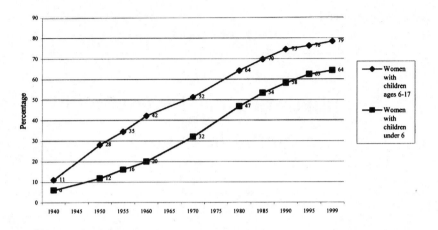

FIGURE A.2   Labor Force Participation Rate of Women with Children, 1940–1999

NOTE: The figure is based on data for 1940 from U.S. Bureau of the Census, *Employment and Family Characteristics of Women* (Washington, DC, 1943); for 1950 to 1955 from U.S. Bureau of the Census, *Historical Statistics of the U.S.: Colonial Times to 1970,* part 1, series D 63–74 (Washington, DC, 1976); and for 1960 to 1995 from U.S. Bureau of the Census, *Statistical Abstract of the United States: 1997,* no. 631 (Washington, DC, 1997); for 1999 from U.S. Bureau of the Census, unpublished tabulations from the Current Population Survey, March 1999 Marital and Family Supplement. Data points from 1940 to 1955 include only married women with children because no data on the employment status of single parents was available for these years. However, during these years, only 2–4 percent of children lived in mother-only families where the mother was employed.

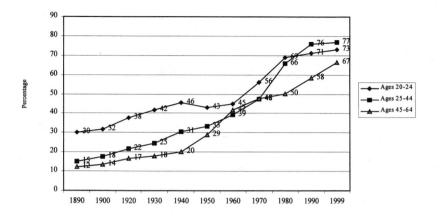

FIGURE A.3 Labor Force Participation Rates for Women Ages 20 to 64, 1890–1999

NOTE: The figure is based on data from the U.S. Bureau of the Census, *Historical Statistics of the U.S.: Colonial Times to 1970*, part 1, series D 29–41, 1890–1970 decennial census (Washington, DC, 1976); for 1980 to 1990 from U.S. Bureau of the Census, *Statistical Abstract of the United States: 1997* (Washington, DC, 1997). The 1999 data points were calculated from data from U.S. Bureau of Labor Statistics, "Employment status of the civilian noninstitutional population by age, sex, and race." Available: http://stats.bls.gov/pdf/cpsa1999.pdf [2000, July 7].

Principal Data Sources

National Survey of Daily Experiences (Daily Diaries Study)

There are four key questions at the core of understanding the obstacles families face. First, how often do work and family responsibilities come into conflict? Second, for whom do the conflicts arise most? More specifically, do both men and women experience them? Are the experiences of poor working families and middle-income working families the same or different? Do young adults experience more or fewer conflicts than older adults? Third, which family members are affected? In particular, is work-family policy all about children, as it is often treated? Are elderly parents and spouses the only other family members involved, or must many other people be considered? Fourth, what types of problems are working Americans helping their family members address? That is, are most work interruptions due to child-care problems or the illness of elderly parents, or is the spectrum of necessity far broader?

These questions can be answered in a range of ways. The easiest way, and thus a common way, to address such questions is to ask people on a survey about their experiences over an extended period. People are asked such things as, how many times in the past year did you miss work in order to care for a family member? The problem with this approach is recall bias.[1] The longer the period of time over which people are asked to recall, the greater the bias.[2] Also, the more common the event, the harder it is to recall the frequency accurately. For instance, most people could more accurately recall the number of hospitalizations they had had in a given year than the number of their minor colds during that time.[3] Daily diaries help to resolve this recall problem by allowing respondents to report on daily events closer to their occurrence.[4]

Together with David Almeida, at the University of Arizona, we conducted the first national daily telephone survey of people regarding their work disruptions to meet family needs. Telephone interviews have been shown to have higher response rates than self-administered questionnaires.[5] Data are recorded more completely in phone interviews than in self-administered diaries because the interviewers can ensure that no questions are skipped. Telephone interviews can also enhance the quality of data because the interviewers can probe incomplete or unclear responses. Finally, phone administration permits rapid feedback about nonresponses, such as missed phone appointments, and thus allows the interviewers to implement special efforts and complete the interviews. For example, interviewers can make extra callbacks to contact a participant who missed an appointment.[6]

We asked a nationally representative sample of 1,031 Americans whether they had had to cut back on their normal activities in the preceding twenty-four hours to help family members meet their needs. The 870 working Americans in this national Daily Diaries Study were telephoned for eight days in a row. When study participants were away from their homes, they were given an 800 number to call and report their experiences. Eighty-seven percent of the respondents completed six or more days. (A truck driver who was on the road working called in from truck stops, and even a participant on a honeymoon called in.) The high quality of the information we obtained owes its greatest debt to the study participants and its second greatest debt to the interviewers.

Over the course of eight consecutive evenings, respondents completed short telephone interviews about their daily experiences. Respondents were asked whether they had had cutbacks on any of their normal activities during the previous twenty-four hours because a family member needed their help. For those respondents who answered yes, follow-up questions were asked to explore what happened and how much it interfered with their work. Open-ended information for each reported cutback was tape-recorded and then transcribed. My research team then coded the information regarding whom the cutback was taken for and why. Coded reasons for taking cutbacks included health needs, school needs, child care, elder care, transportation, instrumental support, emotional support, other support, situations related to divorce, and situations related to a death. Respondents could specify more than one reason. Regarding the person or people for whom a respondent had taken a cutback, the coded categories included own children (either biological, step-, or adopted children), grandchildren or great-grandchildren, other children such as nieces or nephews, parents, spouse or partner, other adults, and multiple generations of individuals. Sufficient data were available to provide detailed coding for 93 percent of responses regarding for whom the cutback was taken and for 88 percent of responses for the reason for cutbacks. Interrater reliability in coding was 99 percent (see Table B.1).

National Longitudinal Survey of Youth (NLSY)

After understanding the magnitude and types of problems families face, we need to understand the resources available to families to meet

220

TABLE B.1 Daily Diaries Sample of Employed Adults

	Percentage of Employed Adults	Percentage of Employed Caregivers[a]	Percentage of Employed Parents
Age			
Mean	46	41	39
Range	25–74	25–70	25–66
Highest education level			
GED, some HS, or less	8	8	8
HS grad.	28	29	30
Some college	27	28	28
Assoc. or bach. degree	26	26	25
Some grad. or grad. degree	12	10	10
Race			
White	90	88	88
Black	6	7	8
Native American	1	1	1
Asian or Pacific Islander	1	1	1
Other	2	2	2
Multiracial	1	1	1
Number of children under 18 in household			
0	56	23	0
1	17	30	40
2	18	32	41
3 or more	9	15	19
Marital status			
Married	64	71	78
Living with a partner	4	4	3
Separated	2	3	3
Divorced	15	15	13
Widowed	4	2	1
Never married	10	5	2
Poverty status			
Above 100% poverty level	92	90	90
Below 100% poverty level	8	10	10

NOTE: Due to rounding, percentages may not always sum to 100.

[a] Caregivers are those who have at least one child under age 18 in the household or are providing eight or more hours of unpaid assistance to a parent or parent-in-law.

their needs. As noted in the text, concrete working conditions—such as the availability of paid sick or vacation leave and of job flexibility—play a critical role in determining whether someone can stay home to care for a sick child, arrange elder care for an aging parent, or take a disabled family member to an appointment with a specialist. I conducted the first studies to take a detailed look at how adults' working conditions vary across the country by social class, as well as the first studies to look at the relationship between the work schedules and working conditions of parents and their children's educational outcomes.

To carry out these studies, the research team I led analyzed data collected by the U.S. Department of Labor on the work schedules and hours, plus the available paid leave and job flexibility, for 4,689 working parents over a six-year period in the National Longitudinal Survey of Youth (NLSY). The NLSY is sponsored by the Department of Labor's Bureau of Labor Statistics and is conducted in collaboration with the Center for Human Resource Research at Ohio State University. The NLSY consists of a nationally representative probability sample of men and women who were 14 to 21 years old when first surveyed in 1979 and who, at the time of my study, were 34 to 41 years old.[7] Women have been observed with their children biannually between 1986 and the present.

Analyzing data collected in the NLSY has several important advantages. First, the NLSY enables us to study directly what resources are available to families. Frequently, surveys examine what benefits companies offer without asking what benefits families receive. At first glance, it might seem that these should be the same thing. However, many companies offer benefits only to some of their employees—for example, to those who have worked for a certain length of time, who are not temporary or part-time workers, or who have a minimum job grade. Thus, company managers might say they offer paid leave, but a significant number of their employees might not be receiving that leave. The second major advantage of the NLSY is that it allows us to learn accurately what resources are available to working Americans across social class. Many previous studies of working families have interviewed primarily middle-income families. Both because of its inclusion of a nationally representative sample and because for many years it contained an additional oversampling of poor families, the NLSY provides detailed data on the working conditions faced by low-income as well as middle-income working families. Third, the NLSY allows us the most detailed examination of the working conditions faced by high-need as well as resource-poor families. Parents who have a child with a chronic health problem, learning disabilities, or behavioral or emotional problems face greater demands on their time. The NLSY conducts detailed developmental and educational examinations of children, in addition to collecting information on health, behavioral, developmental, and educational problems (see Table B.2).

The Survey of Midlife in the United States (MIDUS)

While concrete working conditions are critically important, they tell only part of the story. The attitudes of supervisors and coworkers dramatically influence whether employees can take advantage of available paid leave and flexibility to meet the needs of family members. Of equal importance is the support that family, friends, and neighbors offer employees who need to fulfill caretaking responsibilities. As an associate of the MacArthur Foundation Network on Successful Midlife Development, I focused on examining the conditions working families face across social class, gender, and age groups. The members of our network, consisting of researchers from across the United States and Europe, conducted the Survey of Midlife in the United States (MIDUS), which involved a nationally representative sample of 2,130 employed adults aged 25 to 74 and 1,100 employed adults caring for children, parents, or parents-in-law. The survey included both a tele-

TABLE B.2   National Longitudinal Survey of Youth Sample of Employed Parents

	Percentage of Five-Year Sample of Employed Parents
Age	
Mean	35
Range	31–39
Highest education level	
GED, some HS, or less	17
HS grad.	58
Some college/assoc. degree	8
BA/BS degree	13
Some grad. or grad. degree	4
Race	
White	43
Black	27
Native American	3
Asian or Pacific Islander	1
Other	26
Multiracial	1
Number of children under 18 in household	
0	0
1	26
2	45
3 or more	30
Marital status	
Married	74
Living with a partner	6
Separated	4
Divorced	9
Widowed	1
Never married	7
Poverty status	
Above 100% poverty level	89
Below 100% poverty level	11

NOTE: Due to rounding, percentages may not always sum to 100.

phone interview and a lengthy written questionnaire. In MIDUS, we collected information on working conditions, work-family interactions, relationships with coworkers and supervisors, and workplace and outside support. Among other subjects, MIDUS explored the degree of job autonomy each respondent had. The respondents were asked how often they could decide how to accomplish their tasks at work, determine what tasks to do, plan their work environment, and make decisions about work in general. These aspects of the work environment generally are not measured well or at all in other surveys. Data were collected in MIDUS on the extent to which working adults could rely on family, friends, and neighbors for help (see Table B.3).

Urban Working Families Study

National surveys can answer certain questions better than any in-depth ethnographic study. Such surveys are the best way to determine how many people are affected, how common a problem is, and how frequently people have resources available. But only in-depth studies can fully examine the realities that specific working Americans and their families face. I led the Urban Working Families Study in which my research team conducted more than two hundred in-depth interviews of working families, child-care providers, and employers. In this study, we interviewed a random sample of families who were using a city's pediatric services (see Table B.4). In addition, the medical records of children were carefully reviewed. Families were eligible for this study if all parents living in the household had worked at least twenty hours per week for at least six months during the preceding year. Eighty-two percent of parents who were invited to participate in this representative sample agreed to participate, and 95 percent of those who agreed to participate completed both the closed-item survey and the in-depth, semistructured interview. Nonrespondents were asked a brief series of demographic questions to determine whether there were any significant differences between those who chose to participate and those who did not. There were no significant differences between respondents and nonrespondents in terms of race, education, health-care coverage, marital status, number of hours worked per week, employment status, age of respondent, age of children, or number of children. Moreover, we

TABLE B.3 Survey of Midlife in the United States Sample of Employed Adults

	Percentage of Employed Adults	Percentage of Employed Caregivers[a]	Percentage of Employed Parents
Age			
Mean	44	40	39
Range	25–74	25–70	25–66
Highest education level			
GED, some HS, or less	8	7	7
HS grad.	26	28	28
Some college	25	26	26
Assoc. or bach. degree	27	27	26
Some grad. or grad. degree	15	12	13
Race			
White	88	87	87
Black	7	7	8
Native American	1	1	0
Asian or Pacific Islander	1	1	1
Other	3	3	3
Multiracial	1	1	1
Number of children under 18 in household			
0	57	17	0
1	19	36	43
2	16	32	38
3 or more	8	15	18
Marital status			
Married	64	71	75
Living with a partner	5	5	4
Separated	3	4	5
Divorced	15	14	13
Widowed	4	2	1
Never married	10	4	2
Poverty status			
Above 100% poverty level	93	92	91
Below 100% poverty level	7	8	9

NOTE: Due to rounding, percentages may not always sum to 100.

[a] Caregivers are those who have at least one child under age 18 in the household or are providing eight or more hours of unpaid assistance to a parent or parent-in-law.

interviewed a supplementary sample of low-income families living in subsidized housing and another sample of unilingual Spanish speakers. In open-ended interviews, families were asked about almost every aspect of the relationship between their work and family lives.

In addition, we conducted in-depth, semistructured interviews of child-care providers at every publicly sponsored preschool and after-school program in the city studied. Child-care providers from private centers and home-based child-care providers were also interviewed. Urban child-care providers caring for both preschool and school-age children were interviewed for this study because they provide a unique source of information regarding whether children are sent to child care or school sick and the impact of having sick children in their care. No previous study, to our knowledge, has interviewed child-care providers on this subject. Child-care providers were asked about the daily care they provided for children and the issues they faced in meeting children's health and developmental needs. In addition, study participants filled out closed-item demographic questionnaires. All interviews were taped, transcribed, and analyzed using segment review and content analyses by multiple readers. Of the thirty-two child-care providers interviewed, 34 percent worked in home-based preschool care, 31 percent in school-age after-school programs, 22 percent in public preschool child-care centers, and 13 percent in private preschool child-care centers. Fifty-three percent of those interviewed worked at centers that were publicly funded; 34 percent at centers that were private, for-profit; and 13 percent at centers that were private, nonprofit.

Finally, a random sample of employers, stratified by firm size, was selected from a complete list of the city's employers. In-depth face-to-face interviews and closed-item surveys were conducted with each employer. Employers were asked about a range of issues related to employees' successes and difficulties on the job, including how extensively family needs affect the workplace, which family needs most affect the workplace, who is affected and how when family needs arise,

TABLE B.4 Urban Working Families: Employed Parents Using City Pediatric Services

	Percentage of Employed Parents
Age	
Mean	35
Range	16–55
Highest education level	
Some HS	4
HS/GED	28
Some college	29
College grad.	13
Some grad. or grad. degree	26
Race	
White	54
Black	26
Native American	1
Asian or Pacific Islander	8
Other	5
Multiracial	5
Number of children under 18 in household	
0	1
1	43
2	38
3 or more	17
Marital status	
Married	57
Living with a partner	4
Separated	8
Divorced	8
Widowed	3
Never married	21
Poverty status	
Above 150% poverty level	60
Below 150% poverty level	40

NOTE: Due to rounding, percentages may not always sum to 100.

and when it is or is not the responsibility of the employer to provide assistance. The employer study had a response rate of 74 percent.

Other Data Sources

Other data sources included the Baltimore Parenthood Study and the National Study of the Changing Workforce. I have described the Baltimore Parenthood Study, the questions we asked in it, and the methods used to analyze the data in a 1999 article in the *Archives of Pediatrics and Adolescent Medicine*.[8] Information on the National Study of the Changing Workforce, a publicly available data set we analyzed to examine gender and class differences, is available from the Families and Work Institute in New York or at http://www.familiesandwork.org/announce/nscwcd.html.

NOTES

1. S. Shiffman and A. Stone, "Ecological Momentary Assessment: A New Tool for Behavioral Medicine Research," in *Technology and Methods in Behavioral Medicine*, ed. D. Krantz, A. Baum, et al. (Mahway, NJ: Erlbaum, 1998), 117–131.
2. N. Schwarz, "Self-Reports: How the Questions Shape the Answers," *American Psychologist* 54 (2): 93–105 (1999). A. Stone, R. Kessler, and J. Haythornthwaite, "Measuring Daily Events and Experiences: Decisions for the Researcher," *Journal of Personality* 59 (3): 575–607 (1991).
3. Schwarz, "Self-Reports."
4. Stone, Kessler, and Haythornthwaite, "Measuring Daily Events and Experiences."
5. D. Dillman, *Mail and Telephone Surveys: The Total Design Method* (New York: Wiley, 1978).
6. Stone, Kessler, and Haythornthwaite, "Measuring Daily Events and Experiences."
7. Bureau of Labor Statistics, U.S. Department of Labor, *NLS Handbook, 1999* (Washington, D.C.: Government Printing Office, 1999).
8. S. Heymann, S. Toomey, and F. Furstenberg, "Working Parents: What Factors Are Involved in Their Ability to Take Time Off from Work When Their Children Are Sick?" *Archives of Pediatrics and Adolescent Medicine* 153 (8): 870–874 (1999).

Appendix C

Parental Working Conditions and Children's Educational Outcomes

TABLE C.1   Relationship Between Parental Evening Work and Children's Academic Achievement on Math PIAT

Stepwise Regression Model Controlling for	Odds Ratio for Evening Work
Family income	1.18
Parental education	1.16
Marital status of parents	1.16
Child's gender	1.16
Total number of hours worked by parent	1.17[a]

NOTES: The above table is based on multivariate regression analyses we conducted with data from the NLSY.

[a] For every hour a parent works between 6:00 and 9:00 P.M., his or her child is 1.17 times as likely (or 16 percent more likely) to score in the bottom quartile on math tests. This is the case even after taking into account family income, parental education, marital status, the child's gender, and the total number of hours the parent worked. This finding was statistically significant, with $p < 0.03$.

TABLE C.2   Relationship Between Parental Night Work and Probability Child is Suspended from School

Stepwise Regression Model Controlling for	Odds Ratio for Night Work
Family income	2.91
Parental education	2.91
Marital status of parents	2.71
Child's gender	2.73
Age of child	2.72[a]

NOTES: The above table is based on multivariate regression analyses we conducted with data from the National Longitudinal Survey of Youth.

[a] The children of parents who work nights are 2.72 times as likely (172 percent more likely) to have gotten into trouble and been suspended from school. This is the case even after taking into account family income, parental education, marital status of parents, child's gender, and age of child. This finding was statistically significant, with $p = 0.007$.

Appendix D

Poverty and Working Conditions

TABLE D.1   Essential Benefits, by Income

	Not Poor	Poor	p Value
Lack of paid leave and flexibility			
Lack paid sick leave			
None of the time	45	23	
Some of the time	31	31	
All of the time	24	45	< 0.001
Lack paid vacation leave			
None of the time	64	37	
Some of the time	23	35	
All of the time	13	28	< 0.001
Lack paid sick and vacation leave			
None of the time	68	40	
Some of the time	21	34	
All of the time	11	26	< 0.001
Lack flexibility			
None of the time	27	22	
Some of the time	48	44	
All of the time	25	34	0.003

TABLE D.1 (CONTINUED)

	Not Poor	Poor	p Value
Lack paid sick and vacation leave and flexibility			
None of the time	81	54	
Some of the time	15	33	
All of the time	4	13	< 0.001
Limited paid leave			
Percentage with two weeks or less of paid sick and vacation leave			
None of the time	42	13	
Some of the time	35	32	
All of the time	23	55	< 0.001
Families with adequate benefits			
Percentage with paid sick and vacation leave, and flexibility			
None of the time	47	66	
Some of the time	40	26	
All of the time	13	8	< 0.001
Percentage with at least 4 weeks of paid leave			
None of the time	41	77	
Some of the time	38	18	
All of the time	21	4	< 0.001

NOTE: The table is based on analyses we conducted using data from the National Longitudinal Survey of Youth.

TABLE D.2 Parents' Decision Latitude at Work by Income

	At or Below 150% of the Poverty Line	Above 150% of the Poverty Line	p Value
Do not have a choice in how their job is done	11	6	0.02
Do not have a choice in what jobs are done	26	17	0.01
Do not have a say in planning their work environment	30	18	< 0.001
Do not have a say in decisions about their work	23	13	0.004

NOTE: The table is based on data we collected in the Survey of Midlife in the United States.

TABLE D.3 Parents in Multiple Jeopardy, by Income

	Not Poor	Poor	p Value
Parents who are single, no grandparents, no paid sick leave or vacation			
None of the time	93	61	
Some of the time	6	25	
All of the time	0.8	13	< 0.001
Parents who are single, no grandparents, no paid sick leave or vacation, no flexibility			
None of the time	96	71	
Some of the time	4	22	
All of the time	0.4	8	< 0.001

NOTE: The table is based on analyses we conducted using data from the National Longitudinal Survey of Youth.

TABLE D.4 Working Conditions and Social Supports, by Income

	At or Below 150% of the Poverty Line	Above 150% of the Poverty Line	p Value
Social support outside of work			
Do not feel you can rely on family for help	20	11	0.005
Do not feel you can rely on a friend for help	24	20	0.05
Do not feel you can rely on a neighbor for help	29	13	< 0.001
Double jeopardy			
Bad working conditions and no outside support	8	2	< 0.001
Support at the workplace			
Do not receive help and support from coworkers	13	9	0.008

NOTE: The table is based on data we collected in the Survey of Midlife in the United States.

Appendix E

Earnings Disparities

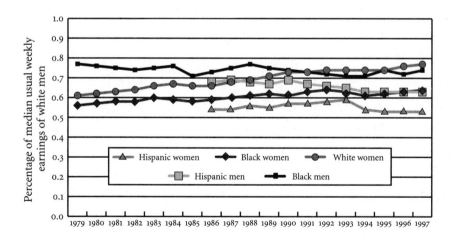

FIGURE E.1   Earnings Disparities, by Gender and Race

NOTE: The figure is based on data from U.S. Department of Labor, Women's Bureau, *Equal Pay: A Thirty-Five Year Perspective* (Washington, DC, 1998).

Appendix F

Caregiving Among Employed Americans

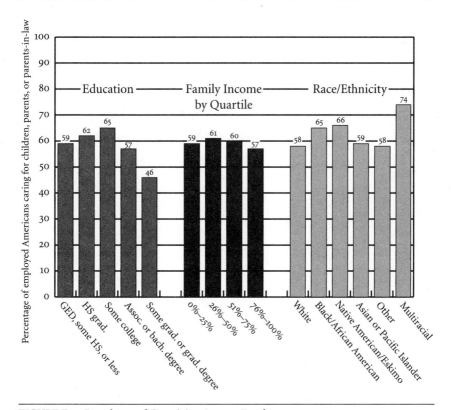

FIGURE F.1   Prevalence of Caregiving Among Employees

NOTES: The figure is based on data we collected in the Survey of Midlife in the United States.

A caregiver is a person who provides at least eight hours per month of unpaid assistance to a parent or parent-in-law or has at least one child under age 18 who lives in his or her household at least part of the year.

Change in School Year
and Ages Taught in Perspective

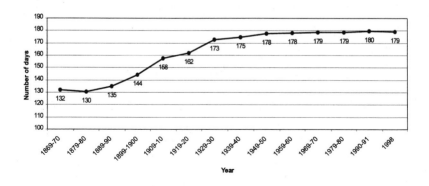

FIGURE G.1   Average Length of School Year (in days), 1870–1998

NOTE: The figure is based on data from the National Center for Education Statistics, *Digest of Education Statistics 1997*, "Table 39: Historical summary of public elementary and secondary school statistics: 1869–70 to 1994–95," available: http://nces.ed.gov/pubs/digest97/d97t039.html [2000, June 29]; and, for 1998, from the National Center for Education Statistics, *Digest of Education Statistics 1999*, "Table 127: Selected characteristics of eighth-grade students in public schools, by region and state," available: http://nces.ed.gov/pubs2000/digest99/d99t127.html [2000, June 29].

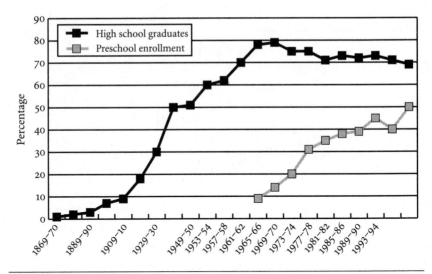

FIGURE G.2   High School Graduation and Preschool Enrollment Rates, 1870–1996

NOTE: The figure is based on data for preschool enrollment from National Center for Education Statistics, *Digest of Education Statistics 1997*, Washington, DC, Table 6, p. 15. Available: http://nces.ed.gov/ pubs/digest97/d97t006.html [2000, June 29]. For high school graduation, from National Center for Education Statistics, *Digest of Education Statistics 1997*, Washington, DC, Table 99, p. 108. Available http://nces.ed.gov/pubs/digest97/d97t099.html [2000, June 29].

Acknowledgments

This book would not have been possible without the generous gift of time made by thousands of families across the country whom we interviewed. Already busy caring for their families while working, they cared enough about getting the voices of America's working families heard that they took time to answer often-lengthy interviews.

Research projects of this magnitude do not happen without the shared vision and support of foundations and other funders. The William T. Grant Foundation generously supported four years of my work examining how parental working conditions affect children's development. The National Institute of Child Health and Human Development generously provided five years of support for examining how parental working conditions affect children's health. The John D. and Catherine T. MacArthur Foundation, through its support of the Network on Successful Midlife Development, made it possible to conduct primary research involving surveys of thousands of adults ages 25 to 75 across the country. The Commonwealth Fund, through an invaluable Picker scholarship, enabled me to conduct the in-depth ethnographic research in the Urban Working Families Study. Funding from the Children's Studies Initiative at Harvard, supported by the Carnegie Foundation, made it possible for me to look at the special needs of children with learning disabilities. Finally, generous support from the Canadian Institute for Advanced Research has freed up my time so that I could pull everything together.

The many research projects described in this book, like all large research projects of which I am aware, were the work of a collective. For the past seven years I have created and led a research group comprising project coordinators, research assistants, graduate students, and undergraduates. This work is truly the product of the deep commitment of many of them, their willingness to fill the multiple roles needed to get the research done, and their insights, creativity, and good humor. Cara Bergstrom, Lisa Berk, and Christine Kerr helped coordinate the research. Together with Maria Palacios and Bora Lee, they did the wide-ranging staff work behind these projects. This work owes an enormous debt to all of them. Alison Earle began working on several of the research projects reported here as a graduate student and then continued as a postdoctoral research associate and a colleague; her attention to detail and depth of understanding of the subject matter have been invaluable. She has had the remarkably able assistance of Nitzan Shoshan.

Several people helped conduct interviews in the in-depth ethnographic studies that composed our Urban Working Families Study: Maren Batalden, Cara Bergstrom, Melissa Dimond, Alison Earle, Meg Hargreaves, Julie Paik, Carl Pallais, and Phuong Vo. Numerous students assisted in ways ranging from reviewing medical charts of children, to transcribing interviews so that the voices of families could be heard in their own words, to collecting data from around the country on programs currently serving working families, to conducting literature reviews and fact checks. These students included Caroline Cruz,

Samantha Dunn, Maurice Jeter, Elizabeth Lowenhaupt, Sonya Merrill, Deanne Nakamoto, Jason Phillips, Uyen-Khan Quang-Dang, Deborah Quint, Christa Van der Eb, and Eijean Wu. The Daily Diaries Study of working families was made possible because David Almeida, who was heading the overarching National Study of Daily Experiences, believed in its importance and was generous with his own and his staff's time to incorporate the research questions. On my research team, Susan Collins, Alison Earle, Elena Li, Nitzan Shoshan, and Sara Toomey contributed to the Daily Diaries Study. Throughout this project, the tremendous support, advice, and insight of researchers with decades more experience than I, have made an important difference in my life and in the quality of the work. I am particularly indebted to, among many others, Lisa Berkman, Bert Brim, Paul Cleary, Harvey Fineberg, Frank Furstenberg, Barbara Gutman-Rosenkrantz, Clyde Hertzman, and Richard Zeckhauser.

All academics should be fortunate enough to have a good editor on projects about which they care deeply. I was blessed with two: Jo Ann Miller and Sharon Sharp. Together, they brought an extraordinary blend of expertise in the subject area and in editing, and a sense of urgency mixed with patience that have greatly enriched the book.

As a working parent, I could not have completed this book without the invaluable efforts of child-care providers, centers, and after-school programs—a patchwork over the years—that have made it possible for me to nurture my sons while continuing to work. Finally, it would have been next to impossible and far less worthwhile without the support of my family. They were supportive in countless ways, from talking through ideas, to providing child care in a pinch, to just believing in the project.

The importance of what we do as a nation for working families has been brought home to me countless times by the unpredictable demands and wise questions of my sons, Benjamin and Jeremiah. This book is dedicated to them and to their generation.

Index

A NOTE ABOUT THE TYPE

The text of this book has been set in Minion, a typeface designed by Robert Slimbach. Released in 1989 by Adobe Systems, Inc., Minion is inspired by the classic, old style type of the late Renaissance. Despite its historic underpinnings, the Minion family is a thoroughly original design, optimized for modern printing methods. The type derives its name from *minion*, a printing term denoting a letter of intermediate size between *nonpareil* and *brevier*.